PRESENTED TO:

_____

FROM:

_____

DATE:

_____

TEACHERS

LIVING A LIFE TO INSPIRE...

GOD'S
WAY

WHITE STONE BOOKS
LAKELAND, FLORIDA

08 07 06 05 04   10 9 8 7 6 5 4 3 2 1

TEACHERS—LIVING A LIFE TO INSPIRE...GOD'S WAY
ISBN 1-59379-016-3
COPYRIGHT © 2004 JOHN M. THURBER
THURBER CREATIVE SERVICES, INC.
TULSA, OKLAHOMA

EDITORIAL DEVELOPMENT AND LITERARY REPRESENTATION BY
MARK GILROY COMMUNICATIONS, INC.
6528 E. 101ST STREET, SUITE 416
TULSA, OKLAHOMA 74133-6754

PUBLISHED BY WHITE STONE BOOKS, INC.
P.O. BOX 2835
LAKELAND, FLORIDA 33806

INTRODUCTION

*"For I know the plans I have for you," declares the Lord, "plans to
prosper you and not to harm you, plans to give you hope and a future."*

JEREMIAH 29:11 NIV

God is faithfully at work today in the lives of teachers—and the
young people they help shape—by revealing His ways, demonstrating
His power, and expressing His infinite love. He is helping teachers
face and overcome incredible challenges, while they set a higher
standard for both colleagues and students by living lives of integrity
and faithfulness.

Are you looking for answers to the many situations you deal with
as a teacher?

Perhaps you are facing pressures with the mounting responsibilities
all teachers uniquely carry.

God's Way for Teachers is filled with true and personal stories
from teachers just like you who have experienced the same issues and
situations you face; teachers who have looked to God for encouragement and spiritual renewal—and received it.

As a teacher you invest high levels of energy into the educational
and emotional needs of your students. Now is your moment to
receive. Prepare to encounter new levels of strength and grace in your
life as you discover what it truly means to live and teach...*God's Way.*

CONTENTS

TEACHERS
LIVING A LIFE TO INSPIRE...

GOD'S
WAY

TEACHING TO CHANGE LIVES

DR. C. GRANT ENDICOTT

Anything is possible if you have faith.

MARK 9:23 TLB

I struggled terribly in school. I did not like school, and it did not like me. Or so I thought. My behavior was horrible, and my reading skills were even worse. Consequently, the school officials placed me in the Remedial Reading Program. Even as I write this essay, I can still feel the chill that came over me when the wooden speaker box would crackle and notify everyone that all the "dummies" should go to the library for special instruction. I remember slipping quietly out of the room, wishing that God would make me invisible.

Although I am sure that "dummies" was not the precise term used, this is exactly what I heard. This daily humiliation, coupled with the call each morning for all those taking "free lunch," was critical in the construction of the emotional wall behind which I hid during most of my adolescence. I was overweight and unattractive. In addition, I was extremely poor. I felt as if life had dealt me a losing hand. I had absolutely no hope that my life would get better. I was beginning to believe that I was destined to be a failure. I longed to be valued, to be someone's "favorite," to be significant.

As a result of these early experiences, I became bitter. I determined to be accepted even if it meant being accepted by the group known only because of their bad behavior. I cannot speak for every child who has had similar experiences, but I can speak for myself. I would have been just as enthusiastic about behaving and learning as I was about misbehaving and refusing to learn if I had only had just one teacher or one principal who made me feel as if I truly mattered.

All that changed when I was moved to Miss Hiter's sixth-grade class. I had always hated the first day of school. I detested meeting a new teacher, and I especially despised going through all the red tape necessary to arrange "free lunch" and Remedial Reading Classes. My mother's habit was to get us to school extra early on the first day to ensure that everything was taken care of exactly as the school required.

To my surprise, I liked Miss Hiter the very first time I saw her. She greeted me as if I were someone significant. She did not seem to care that I was overweight and unattractive. I was certain that she had heard about me. All the other teachers had. They had always made a point sometime during that first week of school to let me know that they simply were "not going to put up with my typical bad behavior in *their* classes."

Miss Hiter, however, was different. She walked to the door and shook my mother's hand. Even though Miss Hiter was at least three inches taller than Mother, she seemed to be looking up at her. After she finished greeting my mother, she turned to me. With her arm around my shoulders, she walked me into the class. She allowed me to sit anywhere I chose. I walked straight to the back, though I was certain that I would end up in the front row before the week was over.

On the second day of that school year, I knew that I truly loved Miss Hiter. At 9:05 Tuesday morning, the speaker crackled much as it had the past five years. I heard the principal clear his throat and call the name of each student who was to report for Remedial Reading in the "Learning Center." When my name was called (I was the only dummy in my class), I sat there and acted as if I did not hear it. Miss Hiter looked straight at me but did absolutely nothing!

After about ten minutes, the principal again cleared his throat and, for the second time, called my name to go to the dummy class. "Grant Endicott, please report to Mrs. Allen's remedial room immediately." I did not move. Miss Hiter was looking straight at me. She took out a pink piece of paper. She wrote a few paragraphs and told Danny Pack, my best friend, to take it to the office. Danny took the paper and looked at me. I could not believe it. She was going to use my best friend to report me to the office. She was just like all the other teachers.

I waited and waited, but the principal never came. Instead, Danny returned with a note for Miss Hiter. She smiled at me. Then she did the most amazing thing—something no teacher had ever done. She winked at me. I loved Miss Hiter. With that one wink, she had spoken a million words of comfort. It was as if she had said, "I know you are hurting, and I am going to help."

At the end of the day, she asked me to stay after class. I was confused. I knew that I had been on my best behavior. After all, she had winked at me. To my dismay, she asked me to sit down and pulled up a chair beside me. Out of her desk, she took a dog-eared old book. She asked, "Do you like horses, Grant?" *Did I like horses? Yes, I liked horses!* Just that last summer my dad had purchased a pony for me at the auction for only fifteen dollars. He was a pinto, and I named him "Apache" after Little Joe Cartwright's horse.

She opened the book and began reading to me from the *Black Stallion.* For the next thirty minutes, I was totally captivated. Unfortunately, my bus was called, and I had to leave. She smiled and told me that she could read to me again the next day. She patted me on the back—and for the second time that day, she winked at me.

I could not wait until the next day. I had never looked forward to school, but I did now. The next morning, Mom did not have to stay after me to get up. I was up and headed for the bus stop in a flash. At the end of the day, I sat down by Miss Hiter, and this time she pulled out two books. One was the old, tattered version from which she had read the day before; the other was a brand-new one. She placed the new book in my hands. I gave it back and told her that I did not have any money to pay for it. She smiled and told me that it was a loaner. That was cool! She said that I had to follow along with her while she read. That was easy enough because she read so well.

After a week or so, we reached half way in the book. That afternoon I went straight to my spot, took my book out, and was ready to follow her with my ruler. She walked over, put her hand on my shoulder, and told me that it was my turn to read to her. Suddenly, my heart jumped in fear. I told her that I could not read well. She smiled and asked me to try—try just for her. At that moment, I would have jumped right out of the window for Miss Hiter. Slowly, I began to read. Before I knew it, two more weeks had passed; and I was turning the last page of my first novel. I shut the book and just looked at it. I had never read an entire book before.

Miss Hiter stood up and started clapping. She really did. Then she turned and picked up another book from her desk. It was the second in the *Black Stallion* series. She handed it to me, and I am almost certain that I saw a tear run down her cheek. For the next eight months, with few exceptions, I read every afternoon to Miss Hiter. As soon as I would finish one volume, she would give me another. Meanwhile, my reading grades continued to improve. Not only did my reading grades get better, but my science and history grades improved as well. By the end of the year, I was nearly the best reader in my class. Well, anyway, that is what Miss Hiter told my mother.

On the final day of that school year, I was the last student to leave. My father always picked me up on the last day, so I had a few extra minutes. I had bought Miss Hiter a gift, a silver apple, from the local dime store. On the apple the clerk had inscribed these words: "Thanks for teaching me to read." I took the personally wrapped gift and set it in front of Miss Hiter.

She raised her head with genuine surprise. She smiled really big and tore away the wrapping paper, which was nothing more than a brown grocery bag.

When she finally opened it, she set it on the desk in front of her and just looked at it. Then she did the most surprising thing. She stood up, walked around her desk, and hugged me. I do not remember any teacher hugging me before that moment. I felt the warmth of a tear as it dropped from her cheek onto my face. I started to cry. Twelve years old and I was crying like a baby. Wow—the amazing power of affirmation! There is nothing like the appropriate touch from someone you love and respect. She could have easily hugged Mitch or Greg or Charles. They were the "good" boys. But she hugged *me*. For the first time that I can recall, I felt really treasured.

I do not know how long I stood there with Miss Hiter. When my father knocked on the door, I turned to leave. As I reached the door, I glanced back and saw that she was getting something from behind her desk. It was a long box. She looked at my father and asked him if she could give me a gift. He gave an affirmative nod, and she put the box in my arms. Inside the box was the entire set of the *Black Stallion* novels.

Everything changed for me that summer. I felt good about myself. I was not a dummy. I lost weight. I entered the seventh grade ready to start a new journey that one day would end in a classroom—my classroom. Miss Hiter moved away that summer. She will never know the impact that she has had on my life.

More than twenty-five years have passed since that first day of my sixth-grade year, but I can still remember vividly how important Miss Hiter made me feel. Although I did not realize it at the time, I had learned an important lesson. I learned that all of us have the power to make someone else feel important. We each can take a terribly bad day in someone's life and make it better, simply by giving an encouraging word or a soft, compassionate smile. Miss Hiter did that for me. Even when she had to scold me, I still knew that she believed in me.

One teacher made all the difference in my life. I am committed to giving to other boys and girls the same love and affirmation that she demonstrated to me. If students know nothing else about me, they will know that I love them. As I go about my daily responsibilities, I find myself looking for that child who sits alone during recess. I look for such a child to put on the cover of brochures and yearbooks.

My passion for students and my commitment to them is a result of my ability to identify with their pain. Because of my past experiences, I am committed to providing children with an environment in which they feel valued, significant, and free from organizational insensitivity. I want to make sure that both the manner and the process of their education preserves their dignity and self-worth. I never want a child to be made to feel like a failure.

Today I have an undergraduate degree, a master's degree, and am presently working to complete my doctoral program. Whenever I reflect on my personal accomplishments, I do not think about my high school or college experiences. As helpful and beneficial as these were, I think about Miss Hiter's sixth-grade class. Thank you, Miss Hiter. You certainly taught from the heart and changed lives...especially mine.

EIGHTEEN YEARS LATE

MICHAEL T. POWERS

He who heeds discipline shows the way to life, but

whoever ignores correction leads others astray.

PROVERBS 10:17 NIV

Junior high is probably the hardest time in young people's lives. Bodies are changing, and a great deal of time is spent trying to fit into a mold that peers have formed for them. Gone are the days of Elmer's glue, crayons, and the tiny scissors with the rounded edges. (Yes, they are trusted with the sharp-edged scissors in junior high.) From here on out, these young adults have their own lockers, carry their books to each class, and start making their own decisions about which classes to take. Oh yeah, I almost forgot. They have to take showers in front of their peers! Naked!

What I remember most about junior high, however, was the incredible pain and heartache that students inflicted on one another with their words and actions. There were students who seemed to have it all together and made those around them feel as if they didn't measure up. It wasn't until much later that I learned that those who ripped on others suffered from a terrible self-image, so in order to make themselves feel better, they tore others down. In fact, they were usually a totally different person from the one they presented to the outside world.

I didn't have the best self-image in junior high, and there were two things that I fell back on to be accepted: athletics and humor. I have always been a decent athlete, which brought a certain confidence and comfort level in my life, and I have always been able to make people laugh. At times the laughter came at another's expense, unfortunately, and most times I didn't fully realize what I was doing to the self-image of those around me, particularly a classmate named Tracy.

She had a crush on me. Instead of nicely letting her know that I wasn't interested in her, I got caught up in trying to be funny, with her being the brunt of my jokes. I am ashamed now to think of how I treated her that seventh grade year. I went out of my way to make things miserable for her. I made up songs about her and even wrote short stories in which I had to save the world from Tracy, the evil villain.

That all changed about halfway through the year, however. Mr. Greer, my physical education teacher, came up to me one day.

"Hey, Michael, you got a second?"

"Sure, Mr. Greer!" I said. Everybody loved Mr. Greer, and I looked up to him like a father.

"Michael, I heard a rumor that you were going around picking on Tracy."

He paused and looked me straight in the eye. It seemed like an eternity before he continued.

"You know what I told the person I heard that from? I told them it couldn't possibly be true. The Michael Powers I know would never treat another person like that, especially not a young lady."

I gulped, but said nothing.

He gently put his hand on my shoulder and said, "I just thought you should know that."

Then he turned and walked away without a backward glance, leaving me to my thoughts.

That very day I stopped picking on Tracy.

I knew that the rumor *was* true, and that I had let my role model down with my actions. More importantly, though, it made me realize how badly I must have hurt this girl and others for whom I had made life difficult.

It was probably a couple of months later before I fully realized the incredible way in which Mr. Greer had handled the problem. He not only made me realize the seriousness of my actions, but he did it in a way that helped me to save some of my pride. My respect and love for him grew even stronger after that.

I don't think I ever apologized to Tracy for my hurtful words and actions. She moved away the next year, and I never saw her again. While I was very immature as a seventh grader, I still should have known better. In fact, I did know better, but it took the wisdom of my favorite teacher to bring it out into the light.

So, Tracy, if you're out there, I am truly sorry for the way that I treated you, and I ask for your forgiveness—something I should have done eighteen years ago.

And to you, Mr. Greer—thanks.

EARBOOK DAY

GINGER COX

And we know that God causes all things to work together for good to

those who love God, to those who are called according to His purpose.

ROMANS 8:28 NASB

Yearbook Day in a middle school can easily become a lost instructional day in the hysteria of the annual excitement. Often without success, teachers strive to focus middle schoolers' attention on their studies, in spite of the countdown to the afternoon's yearbook unveiling. If you remember your own high school yearbook excitement, just multiply it by ten for the wild anticipation of a middle school student's first yearbook.

When I worked as library media specialist at Cowpens Middle School, the principal instructed all teachers to keep their classes on task throughout the morning, and then the afternoon would be devoted to a school-wide assembly and signing parties. After the assembly and yearbooks were issued, each grade was assigned a different area of the campus, which helped with supervision and allowed each grade to have its own celebration. With summer just around the corner, it often became a preliminary "farewell" party, too.

Of course, there are always a few students who are unable to purchase yearbooks. I've seen some compassionate teachers provide blank "Memory Books," so those not having yearbooks could make their own autograph books. They tried to make the day extra special for everyone.

In May of 1997 the morning began as a typical Yearbook Day with the teachers feverishly pushing their students to complete their studies. The principal's voice through the PA system resounded, "Teachers, please remind your classes of our high expectations for exemplary behavior today."

Mrs. Polly Hembree, one of our master teachers and chairman of the language arts department, addressed her class—"Today is a special day to remember this school year. I know you are very excited about receiving your annuals. Our principal recognizes how important this day is to you, eighth graders, especially, so he is allowing you to have two hours outside after lunch to sign yearbooks. Let's be very careful about how we sign these yearbooks. Five, ten, or twenty years from now, you will want to read the good and positive things people wrote about you and you'll want others to be proud of their special memories here in eighth grade at Cowpens Middle School. In light of that, do not under any circumstances write something demeaning about your fellow students."

After the school-wide assembly, each grade moved to its designated area. I meandered from grade to grade with my camera, taking pictures of huddled coveys as they wrote secret messages in friends' books and squealed over friends' comments. Some students ran from group to group. Some sat alone, silently looking through their books. Other students waited in line for their teacher to record her blessings for them. These teachers laboriously wrote notes, reflecting on the year to focus on the best traits of each child.

Occasionally I saw a teacher with a pained expression as she struggled for the right words and then saw the expression relax into a smile as an inspiration rescued her. I smiled to myself and moved on, stopping when I heard, "Mrs. Cox, would you write in my book?" After a personal note, I'd write in true librarian style, "Keep on reading this summer!"

Educators are very aware of the separation of church and state, but sometimes there are moments when we relax our caution. This day, conscientious Mrs. Hembree wrote some personal words of affirmation in a student's annual and felt it would be okay to use a worthy Scripture reference. She reasoned that if interested, the student could look up the verse for himself. So she spent her afternoon, dutifully praising students and signing her name, followed by "1 Corinthians 4:13." The school day ended successfully, without any incidents of misbehavior.

Later that evening, as prim and proper Mrs. Hembree began writing a graduation card to a former student, she suddenly realized that she had been writing 1 Corinthians 4:13 all day, when she had intended to write Philippians 4:13. With heart-stopping panic, she screamed for her daughter to bring her a Bible. All day long, she thought she had been referencing the verse that read, "I can do all things through Christ who strengthens me." (NKJV) To her horror, the verse she referenced read, "Being defamed, we intreat: we are made as the filth of the world, and are the offscouring of all things unto this day."

Early the next morning, she sent me a frantic note, asking me to look in the library's reference section to see if another Bible translation would make the verse sound less offensive. I quickly responded that the *New International Version* made it easier reading. It called them—"the scum of the earth"!

Before you jump to conclusions, let me reassure you that this true story has a happy ending. As promised in Romans

8:28, "God causes all things to work together for good to those who love God, to those who are called according to His purpose" (NASB).

Can you imagine the chuckles in heaven when this devoted Christian lady wrote the Corinthians reference? All the students were shocked when Mrs. Hembree asked them to give her their yearbooks so she could correct a mistake. She quickly realized that not a single one of them had looked up the verse.

Many of us learned valuable lessons from Mrs. Hembree that day. The students learned that anyone can make a mistake, even the head of the language arts department who teaches how to write citations. They learned that one should immediately correct a mistake, even if no one has noticed. Several of us realized that this inadvertent error actually encouraged more students to look at a Bible than if her reference had been correct in the first place. As a former perfectionist, I was reminded again that none of us should take ourselves too seriously.

Together, Polly Hembree and I have laughed through various mishaps we've experienced in our educational careers. Yes, God can make anything work for good to those who love Him and are called according to His purpose, and sometimes we can almost hear His laughter as He works through our mistakes.

*W*HEN YOU'VE GOT WHAT IT TAKES

PATRICIA LORENZ

Not many of you should become teachers, my brothers and sisters,

for you know that we who teach will be judged with greater strictness.

JAMES 3:1 NRSV

My four children are grown and gone—though my youngest is still in college. I am continually amazed that the first three have all chosen to become teachers.

Jeanne received her master's degree in art at Yale University and now teaches art at the California College of Art in Oakland, California, and also teaches at Creative Growth, a center where various art forms are taught to physically and mentally challenged adults.

Julia received her degree from the University of Wisconsin, Stevens Point, and is teaching at-risk youth, ages 17-24 in the

> "THE ROLE OF THE TEACHER REMAINS THE HIGHEST CALLING OF A FREE PEOPLE. TO THE TEACHER, AMERICA ENTRUSTS HER MOST PRECIOUS RESOURCE, HER CHILDREN."
>
> —*Shirley Mount Hufstedler*

Fresh Start Program in Portage, Wisconsin. Each of her students earn their high school equivalency diploma under her tutelage.

Michael, a graduate of the University of Wisconsin, Madison, is the assistant director for the UW Marching Band and also teaches orchestra at the university.

Why am I surprised that they've all become teachers? Because I, for one, tried it and couldn't survive. For me teaching was one of the most difficult, stressful, and challenging careers I have ever attempted. I believe in order to be a teacher one must possess something supernatural. Not only buckets full of talent from God Himself, but something else. I don't know what it is exactly. All I know is that I didn't have it.

I'm not a teacher. Unless you count teaching four children the rudiments of walking, talking, bathroom etiquette, swimming, and cleaning up after themselves. Oh, it's true, I do teach writing workshops here and there. But that's not really being a teacher. That's being on stage and gushing for a few hours to a very appreciative audience, all of whom are electric with a yearning to learn. That's flash-in-the-pan easy teaching.

The kind of teachers I mean are classroom teachers, kindergarten through college. Day-in-and-day-out teachers.

Thirty-five years ago I was in the midst of my last year in college studying diligently to become a high school English teacher, even though I never really had the desire to teach. But my mother kept asking me all through college, "What are you going to do with that English degree if you don't teach?" She and Dad were footing half of the tuition, room, board, and book bills, and I was eager to take what seemed at the time to be good advice. So, I began with my education courses. Philosophy of Education, Problems of Teaching English, History and Principles of Secondary Education, Principles of Teaching Grammar—I suffered through them all.

Those courses were the same ones which had inspired many before me to educate generations of youngsters. But I struggled with each and every one of those methods courses. I dreaded student teaching so much that I dropped out before the end of the first week.

I was fearful of going out in the world with nothing in my hand but a parchment diploma and a B. A. degree in English, which hadn't seemed to have prepared me for much else other than teaching. But, I'm glad I reached into the depths of my soul in time and realized that teaching was better left to the more saintly types. Teaching is a profession for the infinitely patient, the inherently just, the abundantly kind, the intrinsically dedicated, and in my humble estimation, the hardest workers God has put on this earth.

When I dropped out of student teaching, one of my professors asked me why I gave up such a noble profession. "It's simple," I said. "I just don't have what it takes."

As each school year ends, and the graduation ceremonies ensue, my heart swells with gratitude to all the teachers who guided me. And I have true appreciation for all the educators who are teaching today, creating young people who will stand for something because they are armed with knowledge.

God bless all the teachers who do have what it takes to reach out and touch others in a way that few people can.

TEACHER AT LAST

EUGENE EDWARDS

(as told to Gloria Cassity Stargel)

Delight yourself in the LORD and he will

give you the desires of your heart.

PSALM 37:4 NIV

January 15, 1993. It was now, or never.

At my shop that wintry afternoon, I pulled on my black overcoat and stepped outside. With my hand on the doorknob, I paused. *Well, Atlas Plumbing Company, I've devoted thirty years of hard work growing into a skilled plumber and you into a successful business. And you've been good to me and my family. But now I must follow my heart.* I shut the door for the last time and hung on it a sign: GONE OUT OF BUSINESS.

Then, feeling about as daring as David when he went out to fight Goliath with only a slingshot, I climbed into my '91 Burgundy Explorer and at age fifty, turned all thoughts toward

35

my lifelong dream of being a schoolteacher. *Lord, You've brought me this far,* I pleaded. *Please don't leave me now, or I'll fail for sure.*

The teacher who taught me the greatest life lessons never would have called himself a teacher. Mr. Roy was my mentor, my role model, way back before either term was popular. Mr. Roy talked with me, asked me questions, just like I was someone special instead of a scrawny little black kid.

I was about six when we found each other over in Mayfield, South Carolina, where I was born. There was a little family-run store in our neighborhood with the American flag waving right next to the Coca-Cola sign above the screen door. Mr. Roy and some other old-timers were usually there, next to the pot-bellied stove, playing a round of checkers and swapping yarns. I'd sidle up to the checkerboard, to "help out" Mr. Roy with his game.

And it was there, at Mr. Roy's elbow, that many of my values and certainly my life goals were born. Not that my parents didn't teach me things. They did. By example they taught me the value of hard work and the importance of having the Lord in your life. But as there were seventeen of us children at home, individual attention was hard to come by.

"Eugene," Mr. Roy said one day, "whatta you want to be when you grow up?"

"A teacher," I blurted out. Then added with a self-conscious swagger, "That's what I wanna be—a schoolteacher."

In a tone which left no room for doubt Mr. Roy responded, "Then be one!"

Mr. Roy could see the pitfalls ahead, however. "Eugene," he said, dead serious as he wrapped one bony arm around my equally thin shoulders, "There will be times when folks will say, 'You can't do that.' Just remember to take that in stride. Then set out to prove them wrong."

His advice might have worked, too, except that during my junior year of high school, my mom passed away. I knew then that my going to college and becoming a teacher was out of the question. Dad needed me to help him care for the younger children. So I took up a trade instead—plumbing.

I recalled another of Mr. Roy's admonitions. "One more thing, Eugene," he'd said. "Whatever you become, whether you're a ditchdigger or a schoolteacher, you be the best you can be. That's all the good Lord asks of us."

By then, Mr. Roy's principles had become my own. I told myself: *If I can't be a teacher, I'll be the best plumber in the business.* And that's exactly what I tried to do for thirty years. I

learned all I could about the trade. Practiced what I believed—
do it right the first time and you don't have to go back.
Eventually I had my own business.

In the early years I even managed to take an off-campus
college course from time to time, but abandoned that effort
when my plumbing business became too demanding. All the
while, though, buried deep in my heart, the dream of someday
being a teacher pulsed on.

It was in 1971 that I was able to send my daughter to
college, and she has been a teacher ever since, currently
teaching third grade in the public school system. *Maybe her
teaching will satisfy my longing,* my subconscious said. *I can
live my dream through her.*

That day came, though, when my long-desired dream would
no longer be denied. *Eugene,* I said to myself, *you've always
wanted to teach. You love kids. You see the great need for adult
role models. You've prayed about it. Why don't you get out
there and see if you can cut it?* And that's when I closed my
shop and set out to find the answer.

Four days later, I started work at Hendrix Drive Elementary
School. Not as a teacher, mind you, but as custodian. I traded
my wrenches and pipe fittings for brooms and paintbrushes
and a 40 percent reduction in pay. I figured the job would be a

good way to get a feel for the school environment, to test the waters, so to speak, to see if I could even relate to the youngsters of today.

Right away, I hit it off with the students. Out in the hallways running the floor polisher, I'd throw them a big high five, and they responded with wide grins and a "five back at you." Soon they were calling me Mr. Edwards, and the principal even let me read to some of the lower grades.

Often I found a youngster propped up against the wall outside his classroom, having been banished there for misbehavior of one kind or another. "Whatza' matter, son?" I'd ask him, truly concerned. After he had related his current infraction of rules and I had emphasized his need to comply, I'd go in and talk with his teacher, smoothing the way for reconciliation and his return to the classroom.

Surprisingly, I made a very fine mediator, maybe because I could put myself in the mind-set of these youngsters. So many—like my young friend Johnny—came from broken homes, being raised by a single mom or by a grandmother. They were hungry for a positive male role model, someone who would show genuine interest in them, show them they were loved. They desperately needed a Mr. Roy in their lives. I wanted to be that one.

I had time to do a lot of thinking, and praying, while I polished those floors. *Why, I have a ministry right here as a custodian. I'm making a difference in these young lives, in being able to encourage them, challenge them. Maybe I don't need to put myself through the rigors of college courses in order to help students. Even Principal Soper called me "an excellent role model."*

But I heard God say to me, *Yes, Eugene, all that is true. Yet, just think how much more effectively you can minister when you combine your inherent skills with proper training.*

All the while, like a long-play recording, I could hear Mr. Roy saying, "Never settle for second best, Eugene. Whatever you become, you be the best you can be." One night I ventured to the family, "Looks like I'm gonna' have to go to college after all."

"Eugene, it's your turn to get that degree you've always wanted," my wife Annette said, throwing her arms around me. "We'll all help you."

"Yeah, Dad," Michael and Monique added, giving me a thumbs-up. "Go for it!"

So I did. In the fall of '94, I signed up for night and weekend classes at the Norcross branch of Brenau University.

I plain had the jitters when I approached those first classes. *Will I be the oldest student there? Am I too old, too tired to learn those tough subjects?* Even months later—during the twenty-mile drive—often I asked myself, *Eugene, do you know what in the world you're doing?*

Working forty hours a week at the school, before long I found myself studying many nights until 1 or 2 A.M., only to get up at 5:30 in order to be at work by 6:30. Often, while cleaning those floors, I carried on a running dialogue with Jesus. *Lord, I'm bone weary. Remind me again that this is something You want me to do. 'Cause I tell you the truth, if it's just my wanting it, I'm about ready to quit.*

In answer, I believe God sent Johnny back to me. Johnny had graduated our school the year before; now he came by to visit and found me about to replace a fluorescent bulb in a hallway fixture. "Johnny, I am so glad to see you!" I said, while giving him a big bear hug. "How're you doing, son?"

"Fine, Sir," he responded, his good manners impressing me beyond measure. "Mr. Edwards," he went on, "I want to thank you for the time you spent with me here, and for caring about me. I never would have made it through sixth grade if it had not been for you."

"Johnny, I am so proud of you," I responded, giving him my undivided attention. "And you're going to finish high school, aren't you?"

"Yes, Sir," he said, his face breaking into a huge smile, "I'm even going to college, Mr. Edwards! Like you!"

I almost cried to think I had influenced him that much. I determined then and there to stick it out with my studies. Johnny was counting on me, as would other Johnnys yet to come.

Now it is early morning—May 3, 1997—a day that will go down in history, my history, certainly. It is pouring rain, but who cares? Today is graduation day!

I'm driving Monique's '96 White Mustang up I-85 north the fifty miles to Gainesville for rehearsal. The family will follow for the ceremony at 10:00. I glance at my hand on the steering wheel and admire the blue-stoned college class ring on this fifty-five-year-old plumber's work-worn finger. On the seat beside me are my black robe and mortarboard with tassel. Out loud I keep saying, *"Praise You, Jesus! Thank You, Jesus."*

The rain has eased up by the time I park at the Georgia Mountain Center where Brenau University's Commencements are being held, this one for Evening and Weekend College Undergraduates. I sit there several minutes, basking in the glow. I can't deny it. Tears of happiness threaten to run down my cheeks.

At the 10:00 ceremony, I am almost overcome with emotion. As the music swells, the processional begins with the university president and faculty in full academic regalia looking impressive indeed, along with trustees of the university and the guest speaker: The Honorable Edward E. Elson, United States Ambassador to the kingdom of Denmark.

All those dignitaries remain standing to honor us as we file in—350 candidates for degrees. When my turn comes, I somehow get up onto the stage to receive my diploma, but I never feel my feet touch the floor!

I float back to my seat, beaming like a lit-up Christmas tree, clutching the tangible evidence of a long-desired dream come true: a square of parchment with those all-important words, Bachelor of Science Degree in Elementary Education.

Yessiree, my inner self is thinking, *just goes to show you. If you dream long enough—and work hard enough—the good Lord will help make your dream come true.*

A teacher at last! Mr. Roy would be proud.

To STACEE WITH LOVE

JOAN CLAYTON

But you have made me very happy....

PSALM 4:7 NCV

Ten years ago I retired from a job that gave me multiple blessings. How I have missed the children. Even today, the sight of a school bus brings back fond memories. My treasure chest is full and running over.

Stacee is one of those memories. She still blesses me today with the joy I saw in my classroom. She brought sunshine to the days when the sand blew and when I had bus duty, playground duty, teachers' meetings, and a headache.

Stacee grasped learning, literally savoring each assignment. She listened attentively to instruction. Her adoring eyes never left mine as they followed me around the classroom. Many times I prayed: *Lord, help me be the kind of teacher Stacee thinks I am.*

Stacee indeed became my teacher. As a second grader, she determined to be happy in life and gave that gift of joy to everyone she met. She wrote me notes every day, and they are all in my "Treasure Book." But more than that, she wrote her notes on my heart. She taught me the real meaning of unconditional love. Who would think I could learn so much from a seven-year-old? She taught me that happiness comes from within, not from external circumstances.

When I told my last class I was retiring, the children cried and said, "Teacher, you don't love us anymore." Stacee consoled the class with her optimistic upbeat attitude, "We can still go to see her. We can still write to her," and so they did, many times, but it was Stacee, her mom, and sister who blessed my husband and me with many visits. It was Stacee who determined to still bring joy to a retiring teacher who missed the children. Always thinking of someone else, Stacee's heart is the happiest because it beats for others.

A bond exists between teacher and student that can never be severed. Students leave footprints on a teacher's heart, and Stacee has permanently left her footprints on mine.

She is destined for greatness. She makes the great moments in her life and doesn't miss a single one.

If I could speak to all of the students I taught over the course of my career, I would want to bless and thank them. My thirty-one years of teaching are filled to running over with wonderful memories. I will miss each one of my students; but the best is yet to be, and "I press on toward the mark." God has sent me children…angels who have grown in the garden of my heart!

Thank you, Stacee, for this wonderful honor. To have had you as a second-grader and now as a graduating senior who has chosen me for the teacher who made the greatest influence upon your life, my heart is filled with unspeakable love and gratitude.

You will forever remain in my thoughts and prayers. I will never forget you, and I will always love you!

*O*UR SEASON OF FAITH

HUGH CHAPMAN

That if thou shalt confess with thy mouth the Lord Jesus,

and shalt believe in thine heart that God hath

raised him from the dead, thou shalt be saved.

ROMANS 10:9

"FAITH IS THE RESPONSE OF OUR SPIRITS TO BECKONINGS OF THE ETERNAL."

—*George A. Buttrick*

Though my career as a banker was financially rewarding, I was never fully content with the work. Compliance regulations, qualification formulas, and credit declinations always seemed so cold and, well…calculating.

It was no wonder that, after only my fourth year on the job, I began to look with envy at the teaching career my wife, Julie, had chosen. Still, to make a career move so late in my life seemed absolutely out of the question. To leave a secure position and return to school was something that would take more faith (and more throwing caution to the wind) than I possessed.

Yet God continued to speak to me through an odd feeling of longing that would often ease into my deliberation. I'd find myself watching Julie as she graded papers until late at night. In the soft lamplight I'd see her smile with satisfaction at the progress of her students and sigh with dismay when they failed to meet her expectations. Though her salary was only half the amount of mine, I knew she was much more gratified in her career than I had ever been. And in time, I began to realize that there must be something more to teaching than I was able to see.

Then one winter evening I found her fretting, in typical fourth-grade teacher fashion, over a student's worsening academic performance. "Baxter will never be a strong student," she said with a sigh, "but at least he used to try. He began the year doing so well, but now his work has dropped to nearly nothing. I just don't understand it."

Two days later the answer became very clear—for both of us.

That evening as I arrived home, exhausted from a hard day at the office, Julie met me at the doorway. "Will you drive me to Baxter's house?" she asked.

I looked at my watch in dismay. It was already getting dark. "Oh, I don't want to bother strangers this late," I whined, "and besides, it's cold out there." But Julie was adamant and promised that she only wanted to drive by to see the house. Reluctantly, I agreed, and together we began our journey.

Baxter's home was at least twenty miles from where we lived, but more than just the distance, the place was hard to find in the dark. We turned off the highway, then rumbled down a rural Arkansas county roadway with only a vague notion as to where we were going. In time, we turned from the graveled road onto a narrow dirt path. My concern was growing by the minute. "You know, some of these folks have shotguns by the door," I said, "and they don't always welcome strangers in the middle of the night."

But my wife was determined. "It's only six o'clock," she said, "and besides, it can't be much farther." Then pointing excitedly, she said, "Look, there it is."

Before us stood an old rundown trailer house, unlit, and barely visible in the mid-winter darkness. In what might have been called a front yard (which was really only a cleared spot in the woods) there were four elementary-aged children. Some were bundled in jackets, others in only their shirtsleeves. Two were busily gathering firewood, one was pouring kerosene into a lantern, and another was petting a mangy old dog. As we pulled slowly forward, a chubby kid in overalls hurried toward the car and enthusiastically greeted Julie. "My mom's not home yet, Mrs. Chapman, so you can't come in. But we can visit out here."

And though my wife did happily chat with the boy for ten minutes, there was really no need to go inside. She had seen what she had come to see; the rundown dwelling of her fourth-grade student and all his siblings—heated with a tiny wood stove and illuminated with two kerosene lamps.

On the quiet drive home, Julie batted back a tear as she softly verbalized what we both had witnessed. "His work was good in the early fall when the days were longer. But now that it gets dark so early, he can't see to do his homework." It was then that I began to understand what she had known all along. Within her classroom my wife had worked to find a means to reach these children—and perhaps to even release them from a life of destitution.

As I drove through the Arkansas night, I watched her from the corner of my eye, and from deep within I realized that I, too, had discovered what God was calling me to do. The only question that remained was whether or not I had the faith to make the change.

What I hadn't counted on was that God had been speaking to Julie, too, and as we discussed the possibilities—tentatively at first, then later more boldly—we began to formulate a plan. By the end of the month, I had said farewell to my friends at the bank.

Then for two and a half years we struggled to make ends meet while I attended college. Eventually, our perseverance paid off, and I was offered my first contract.

I would teach junior high special education in the same district that my wife had been teaching fourth grade.

After my first day I proudly brought forth my new class roster for Julie to see. There among the list of seventh graders was a name that we both recognized: my wife's former student, Baxter. He had found the strength to hang on and had finally made it into junior high—and so had I.

As we began our new venture together, Baxter and I became fast friends. He was a big, friendly kid with a permanently fixed smile, and though his ability was well below many of his classmates, he always gave his very best.

It was disheartening to watch him struggle so hard—producing so little. One evening I shared my dismay with Julie.

"It seems so unfair," I said. "Baxter struggles every day, and I can't seem to help him much. I'm thinking that maybe a more experienced teacher could do a better job."

Julie softly shook her head and replied with a sympathetic smile. "God put you in that classroom with Baxter for a purpose. You might not be able to see it now, but someday you will, you just have to have faith and hang in there."

Her words were encouraging, but I'm afraid her faith was greater than mine. Then something strange happened.

It was nearing Christmastime of that first year, and in the excitement of the upcoming holiday vacation, I was having a hard time keeping the attention of my class. In hopes of making the most of an unruly situation, I assigned an essay: "What Christmas Means to Me."

It was then that Baxter surprised me with his composition.

Though short and ill arranged, it represented, for him, a massive effort. In large block-printed letters and with writing seasoned in a jumble of spelling and punctuation errors, the sincerity of his work was shining through.

WHAT CHRISTMAS MEANS TO ME

Some wise men heard that a new king would be born in Bethlehem, and they made their way through the woods to find him and they followed a star and they came to a barn where the baby was already born. And when they saw him, they knew it was Jesus, and they

bowed down and worshiped Him, because they knew
that the new baby lying in a manger would be the King
of all kings.

I looked to Baxter with a newfound respect as he stood beside my desk waiting, hopefully, for my approval. When I paused to gather my thoughts Baxter quickly pointed out, "There's more on the back."

Pleasantly surprised at the length and the relative accuracy of his effort, I quickly turned over the page to read the conclusion of Baxter's essay.

The wise men were amazed at all they had seen that
night, and while they were walking back to their homes,
they talked about all the great things they had seen. Then,
when they got about halfway home, one of the wise men
turned to the others and said, "Hey, do you know what?
This ought to be a Holiday." And from then on, it was.

Baxter remained at my desk with his simple, friendly smile.

He was not trying to be cute, nor funny, nor insincere.

He was simply reporting an important event in the way he had imagined it to be. And for his honesty, I admired him all the more.

"Baxter," I asked, "do you believe that? Do you believe that Jesus is the Son of God, and that He was sent here to be our Savior?"

Baxter seemed uncomfortable and shifted his weight from one foot to another. Finally he said, "I'm not sure, Mr. Chapman. I go to church sometimes, and that's what they say. But how can you know something like that for sure?"

"You have to have faith that it's true, Bax," I said, pointing to my chest. "And when you have faith, you'll know, because you'll feel it deep inside your heart."

He looked solemnly toward me. "Do you believe it?" he asked.

I nodded assuredly. "I do, Baxter, and very much so."

My student then smiled happily. "Well, if you believe it, then I believe it, too, Mr. Chapman. Because you're real smart, and you know almost everything."

From deep within, I felt his sincerity, but I had to shake my head. "No, Baxter. You shouldn't believe it because I believe it; you should believe it because you feel it from deep within your own heart. That's how you'll know for sure."

As Baxter walked away that day, I experienced a new feeling of purpose, one that I had not known before that moment.

And from my own heart, I knew that I was exactly where God intended for me to be.

It was six weeks later, shortly after the kids returned from Christmas vacation that Baxter approached my desk.

This time he held a small New Testament, open to a well-marked page with a single underlined verse: "For God so loved the world, that he gave his only begotten Son, that whosoever believeth in him should not perish, but have everlasting life."

Excitedly he whispered, "They gave this to me at church, Mr. Chapman, on the day I was saved. They say I can keep it for my own."

Though I shook Baxter's hand and patted his back, there was no way I could express the happiness I felt for the decision he had made.

More than a decade has passed since Baxter entered my first classroom. As a now-seasoned teacher, I've learned that students come suddenly into our care, share a part of our lives, and then often just as quickly, they move on to other things. Occasionally, however, through our time together, our lives are altered forever.

Two years ago at Thanksgiving my family received word that Baxter had been in an automobile accident. Police reports indicated no drinking, no drugs, and no hazardous road conditions—just a single automobile with a single fatality on a quiet, Arkansas highway.

I said a prayer that day for Baxter, but I knew that the important decision had been made long before; an arrangement born of faith within the trusting heart of a determined young man.

Sometimes even now, in the quiet of an early winter's evening, I'll find myself driving along winding country roads. And I'll recall how a boy named Baxter, who through his own faith, exchanged a broken-down trailer house for a mansion on high.

And from deep within my heart I hold to my own faith, the assurance that I will see him again one day; only this time it will be in the company of the King of kings.

And you know what?

A day like that just ought to be a Holiday.

TEACHING IN SOMEONE ELSE'S HOUSE

BRADLEY S. COLLINS

Rejoice with those who rejoice; mourn with those who mourn.

ROMANS 12:15 NIV

In order to make ends meet during my first full-time semester as a college freshman at age forty-three, I held several "on call" positions. In addition to working as a counselor, I was also fortunate enough to be able to substitute teach at the elementary school where my daughter attended fifth grade.

On several occasions, I would receive a call, for various reasons, to stand in for an absent teacher. Through these joyous occasions, I was afforded the opportunity to ride to and from school with my daughter, Whitney, and sometimes even enjoy lunch or other short moments throughout the day with her. What a blessing! Bringing home the bacon (at least a strip or two) and having the great fortune of experiencing more closeness with my daughter.

One afternoon as I was finishing up from a day of "subbing," I was called into the principal's office and informed that the teacher for whom I had filled in for that day, was in the middle of a family crisis. Her father had suffered a stroke and was unconscious. She had decided to take a leave of absence to attend to her father and other family concerns. Administration had asked if I would be willing to stand in for the teacher for speculatively one month with the understanding that the actual time frame requirements were quite unpredictable, at the moment.

While I mentally sifted through my personal calendar to discern as to whether or not I had any pending obligations which might hinder my acceptance of the assignment, I thought about the teacher for whom I was substituting. How fearful, uncertain, and anxious she and her entire family must be.

I thought about her father; he was indeed fortunate to have a daughter who loved him so. She was willing to separate herself from a classroom full of children she had undoubtedly come to love and students for whom she felt a great responsibility. These young ones had come to depend upon her daily presence in their lives. I considered the weight that this decision bore upon her and the anxiety she must be feeling about entrusting her class to a stranger.

I took a moment to pray for the absent teacher's father, in hopes of his full recovery, which did occur. I also remembered to thank God for giving me the opportunity to spend so much time in the presence of Whitney, watching her flourish during those memorable days at school. I was especially grateful when she would take time during her lunch or recess to stop in my classroom, beaming, with one or more of her friends in tow. She would stop in for a quick visit, to just say "hi" and show off her dear ol' dad.

I will never forget that blessed time when I was so profoundly reminded that God never closes a door without opening a window, even if it's in someone else's house.

A TOUGH LITTLE PHILLY IN TEXAS

DARLA SATTERFIELD DAVIS

A gentle answer turns away wrath, but a harsh word stirs up anger.

PROVERBS 15:1 NIV

The first time I saw Terrie's mother, she was irate and being escorted out of our elementary school by two police officers. She was a fireball from "Philly," and our little Texas town had never seen the likes of her.

Parent/teacher conference night was soon to follow, and I was dreading the meeting. I earnestly sought the Lord about it because I was genuinely concerned about Terrie, yet I didn't want to encounter a repeat performance from her mother. The following day I sensed God leading me to handle the conference assertively.

"Hi! I'm Ms. Davis. I've been so anxious to meet you," I said cheerfully as I came from behind my desk to greet her. "Let me close this door so we can really talk."

Before she could start in with her usual discourse, I said, "It is so encouraging when parents care about their kids and keep tabs on them like you do. Now...," I continued, hardly drawing a breath, "I need your advice. After all, no one knows Terrie better than you, right?"

She nodded and sat staring at me.

"I need your input on the best way to handle her when she disrupts class or doesn't complete her assignments." I sat ready to take notes.

Taken aback she stammered a bit before she began listing consequences she felt I could use. She ended by patting me on the knee and assuring me that if Terrie didn't do exactly as I told her, I was to let her know, and she would take care of it.

Things began to turn around for Terrie, and from that day until this, whenever I see her mother, she greets me and begins talking like we are old friends. The wisdom of God works wonders.

LESSON IN GRACE

BOB CHRISTMAS

(as told to Gloria Cassity Stargel)

You must make allowance for each other's faults

and forgive the person who offends you. Remember,

the Lord forgave you, so you must forgive others.

COLOSSIANS 3:13 NLT

It had rained all day in Bedford County, Virginia, and the football field was one massive mud puddle—enough to dampen anyone's spirits. As head football coach of Jefferson-Forrest high school with a Friday night homecoming game at stake, I was wound up tight. Our Cavaliers out on the field seemed to have lost their focus, especially my son, Robby.

Tension had been building all year between Robby and me, since as a junior he had moved up to the varsity team. He played quarterback—the position I coached—and I was plenty hard on him. I wanted my son to make a great football player.

At the same time, I didn't want anyone to accuse me of playing favorites. So I came down heavy. Being a dutiful son, he never argued back. But often in the car or at home after practice, or after a game, a huge wall of silence went up between the two of us—a wall so thick it seemed impenetrable.

Though the night was miserable, the band struck up the school rallying song. The cheerleaders waved their red and white pom-poms, trying valiantly to generate some enthusiasm in the soaked stands and on the soggy field.

I had Robby playing free safety and if I had told him once I had told him a hundred times, when playing free safety there is one thing you never do—"Never let the receiver behind you." The ball was put in play. Robby dropped back. But for some reason he hesitated, hesitated just long enough for the guy to get behind him. The ball went over Robby's head, and the receiver caught the pass. I was livid. From the sidelines I barked, "Robby, get over here!" And so number five dragged himself off the field, looking like a puppy expecting a chewing out. "Stand right there," I scolded, "and don't move a muscle." The fact that I had humiliated my son in front of his team, his peers, and the entire crowd never occurred to me. I was too busy trying to win a ball game.

I knew I was being too tough on Robby, but as the next to oldest of my six children and the first son to play football for me, I wanted him to be the best he could be. Yet, I couldn't seem to separate being his father from being his coach.

Some days later at home, I went into his room and found him crying. I sat beside him on the edge of his bed, a father now, not a coach. "What's the matter, son?"

The floodgates opened as he began to list the hurts I had inflicted on him while playing football. "Dad, you make me the scapegoat. All the time."

"What do you mean?"

"There can be six of us talking while you want us to listen, yet it's always, 'Robby, get quiet.'" Then Robby added with emphasis, "And it isn't said with much grace or mercy."

He wasn't through. "You always put me down, Dad, if I make the slightest mistake. Sometimes, even when someone else makes a mistake. Yet when I do something right, you don't say a word. I feel like nothing I do is good enough for you."

"Robby, I am so sorry I've hurt you." By now, I'm almost in tears. My family is the most important thing in the world to me. I've always tried to be a good Christian influence on them. I didn't realize I had let football affect how I treated my own child.

"I'm beginning to see what happened," I confessed. "I have been so afraid someone would accuse me of favoritism, I went too far in the other direction. Besides that, I guess I hoped that by fussing at you, the others would know what not to do. That was totally unfair." I wrapped my arm around his drooping shoulders, "Will you please forgive me?"

"Dad, I want to be a good football player, as much as you want me to be."

"Yes, Robby, I know that. But because you are my son and I want the best for you, I expected perfection from you. That's too much to ask of anybody."

I did some serious praying that night, asking God to forgive me, too. *Help me, Lord, to be a father who encourages—not one who drives my child to despair.*

I'd like to say I changed overnight. But it took me the rest of Robby's junior year to learn to separate being his dad from being his coach. And truth is, I'm a tough coach. But I tried to be fair about it and stop using Robby as a scapegoat. Not always successfully, I'm afraid.

It didn't help our relationship when I blew it in a big way at the end-of-season football banquet for parents. At the podium, I called out the names of all the players. "Did I leave anyone out?"

"Yes, your son." It was Robby.

Lord, I've failed again. I had to ask Robby to forgive me.

Things weren't much better his senior year—a year that should have been special because now Robby was heir apparent to the star quarterback position. He had a great pre-season. But on the last play of our pre-first-game scrimmage, Robby, 5 feet 5 inches weighing 125 pounds, made a run down field, and some pretty heavy guys piled on him. After they peeled off, he crawled out saying, "Dad, something's wrong with my neck. It hurts."

I insisted he get back in there and finish the possession. He did, and then repeated, "Dad, I'm hurt."

"Okay." I said, "Go see the trainer."

Rob's collarbone was broken! I felt I had failed yet again. Big time.

We both were devastated. The doctor said Robby would be out of the game at least five weeks. It took eight. By then, he had lost his starting position as quarterback and was never able to regain it. When finally his injury allowed him to play again, I'd let him go in the game from time to time. But his season was ruined.

Upon graduation, our tiffs were farther apart since he was no longer playing football for me. However, while attending college, he began coaching with me. Even then, I would forget my professionalism with him from time to time. He learned to come over close and remind me with one word said in that certain tone, "Dad...." I immediately knew I had again crossed the boundary.

Finally, I had the opportunity to clear the air between us. I couldn't change the slights and hurts inflicted in the past. But I was determined to do something I should have done all along.

With both of us as coaches, we were at our first end-of-the-season banquet at North Hall High School in Gainesville, Georgia. Guests came dressed in their Sunday best. Decorations with the school colors of green and white gave the dining hall a festive air. Balloons hung everywhere, crepe paper streamers draped in strategic places, while on the table tiny green footballs perched at each plate and football helmets holding flower arrangements provided centerpieces. All to honor our Trojans who had just finished a winning season.

I took the microphone to introduce our coaches, who in turn would introduce each of their players. When it came Robby's turn, I told the group a little about how he had played for me. "He was a good player," I said, "but he had to put up with a lot from me. Many nights I had to come home and ask his forgiveness for treating him so unfairly. But he's forgiven me, and we've moved on."

I finished with, "Now he's coaching for me, and I have to say, he is one of my best coaches." I turned to where he was sitting, "Robby, great job!"

Robby strode up and accepted my extended handshake. Then he had his own nonprofessional moment—he hugged his head coach. Beaming all the while, I hugged back. And the audience? The audience loved it and burst into enthusiastic applause. There may have even been a few moist eyes as well.

Soon after, my wife Peggy shared something Robby had recently told her. "Mom," he said, "the things I had to deal with while playing for Dad were difficult. He was incredibly hard on me. But, Mom," he went on, "I'll take all that for the experience and honor of playing and learning under the best coach there is."

Thank you, Robby, for extending grace to me in the midst of all my humanness. By your example, I have learned a vital truth—one I needed to know. As humans with human weaknesses, we must be patient with each other just like our heavenly Father is understanding and patient with us. Because of you, Robby, I've gained a better understanding of God's love.

Truly, our experience has been—a lesson in grace.

TEACHERS LIVING A LIFE TO INSPIRE

EILEEN KEY

I thank my God every time I remember you.

PHILIPPIANS 1:3 NIV

I cleaned out my filing cabinets and pitched out purple ditto machine masters as well as internet information. From the old to the new, the wastebasket caught paper after paper as I prepared to retire. Thirty years of teaching school neared an end. No longer would I scrawl an assignment on a chalkboard and face rows of students. The idea was hard to absorb.

As I shuffled through file folders, I came upon one I had kept for encouragement. It contained letters and cards from students and parents I've known. One letter fluttered to the floor. When I bent to retrieve it, I saw Jennifer's name. Tears welled in my eyes, and I reached for the chair.

"MOST OF US END UP WITH NO MORE THAN FIVE OR SIX PEOPLE WHO REMEMBER US. TEACHERS HAVE THOUSANDS WHO REMEMBER THEM FOR THE REST OF THEIR LIVES."

—Andy Rooney

Jennifer came from a broken home. She was a bright red-headed youngster, her face peppered with freckles. As a sixth grader, she still had a tiny lisp, and some of her conversations would embarrass her. She talked to me frequently of her life and brothers and sister. She shared how her mom struggled to work and make her oldest brother behave in school. She couldn't understand why he would want to break the rules. Her heart was incredibly clean and pure.

A fellow teacher and I began a believers' group, and the first students who joined coined the name STAND. Students Taking A New Direction. We met on Friday mornings before school for thirty minutes and had prayer, praise, and fellowship. An array of youth pastors crossed the threshold to give short, motivational devotions.

I mentioned the group to Jennifer, and she became a regular. By eighth grade, she was an officer. Circumstances at home hadn't improved, but her attitude and understanding had. She continually asked for prayer for her family.

Each year eighth graders were given a party in their honor as a send-off to high school. Any who chose to do so had the opportunity to speak about what STAND meant to them. A box of Kleenex was a must.

The year I received this letter, Jennifer was to be the final speaker at the party. She took the microphone in hand, waited a few moments, took a big gulp, and then looked at me. My heart galloped.

"Everybody, I want to tell you something." Another gulp. "I am going to go to heaven. Maybe not today, maybe not for a long time, but I'm going. And, it's all because of my sixth grade English teacher, Ms. Key. You see, she listened to me, and she cared. She didn't just tell me it would be all right. She introduced me to Someone who would make it all right. She told me about Jesus. And, because I know Jesus, I have a reservation in Heaven."

She stepped over, hugged me, and slid a letter into my hand. I read it when I got home. Again, she spoke of my importance to her and thanked me for my investments in her life. I realized although prayer had been outlawed in public schools, Jesus had crossed the barriers.

I've taught many lessons and children over the past thirty years. But knowing that Jennifer has Jesus in her life now…well, that may just be the most meaningful lesson of all.

A HEART THAT LASTS FOREVER

JOAN CLAYTON

And now these three remain: faith, hope and love.

But the greatest of these is love.

1 CORINTHIANS 13:13 NIV

"TO FEEL RICH, COUNT ALL THE THINGS YOU HAVE THAT MONEY CANNOT BUY."

— *Anonymous*

I believe every child in my room was there not by accident, but placed by God. Each one became my forever friend, and I formed a love in my heart that I could never let go. Such was Robert.

He came to my second-grade classroom with his older married sister as an interpreter. He found his name tag and seated himself while placing his supplies just so on his desk.

Those big black eyes told me volumes about him, and his broad smile welcomed me into his young life. He was small in stature but had a big heart; I knew God had sent me another gift.

Robert was the youngest child in a close-knit family. They might not have had much in material possessions, but they were millionaires in love. I relished the interest his older sister took in Robert's accomplishments shown by her frequent visits. His family came to our school many times to admire his work, to smile at me and shake my hand, and always presented me with a good-bye hug. They seemed to appreciate my efforts to dialog with them in broken Spanish.

At the end of the first day of school, I found my first "I love you" note from Robert. Before the school year ended, I had 180 notes from him, a love note for each day. I still have them today.

Robert's superior work and creativity, especially in art, told me a great deal about his future. I relished each day, knowing in my heart I was one day closer to my retirement. Looking back, it was my greatest year. I simply loved the children more than ever, and they seemed to learn more than ever.

Before I knew it, the school year had ended. "This is for you, Mrs. Clayton. I will miss you. I love you." Holding back my tears was not an option. Robert handed me a used Barbie doll with a make-do dress of red and yellow crepe paper that stood in a glass vase. Red ribbons around the vase held two tiny hearts tied with love by little chubby hands. One heart read "Robert," the other "Mrs. Clayton." I wondered if Robert had to sacrifice something he loved to give me this gift. Did he have to trade something he treasured with one of his siblings?

His family also came to tell me good-bye. Robert's dad hugged me and handed me an envelope. Inside was a one-dollar bill with a note: "Un regalo para ti con muchas gracias para enseñar nos hijito." (A present for you with many thanks for teaching our little son.) This time the tears burst into a river. With a widow's mite and a heart of love I had received the gift of all gifts. I still have the dollar and will keep it always.

Robert's parents had supported me all year. We had become close friends as we laughed at my Spanish with a southern accent. I looked forward to seeing them at parent conferences, parties, and other activities, but now the time I had to share in Robert's life would be given to the third-grade teacher. Robert left me with a piece of his heart.

The next year I received many phone calls from Robert. "Mrs. Clayton, this is Robert. I just wanted to tell you. I...uh...well, I...uh, I just want to say, Mrs. Clayton, I just want to say, well....I just want to say, 'I love you.'"

As a third grader Robert called and invited me to an Art Show where his work had won first prize. I beamed with pride as he led me around showing me his creations.

In sixth grade, Robert invited me to his graduating class that would be entering junior high. He made a beautiful speech. He immediately came down the steps to hug his family and me. I cried.

Robert's phone calls were not as frequent after that, and I understood completely. He was growing up, and I thrilled upon reading about his many accomplishments in our local newspaper.

One day in late May I received a phone call. "Mrs. Clayton, I love you." I recognized the voice immediately. "This is Robert. Remember me? I was in your class the year you retired."

"Well, thank you, Robert. After ten years you still remember me?"

"I could never forget you, Mrs. Clayton. I'm calling to see if you could come to my high school graduation. It's Saturday afternoon at 1 o'clock."

"My husband and I will be there and thank you so much!"

We left early since we had to drive a distance to his high school. I told Emmitt about all the wonderful things I remembered about Robert and his family. He could hardly wait to meet them.

We found a seat and began to read our program. Imagine my excitement when I saw Robert's name as "Valedictorian."

Of course that didn't come as a surprise. I had always known his potential.

Robert gave a marvelous valedictory address. He spoke of wonderful heights to be achieved, persistence in seeking the good, and having the determination to never give up. My pride in him could not be measured. He then gave his speech in beautiful Spanish. I loved every minute of it!

After that I heard Robert saying, "Now I want to honor a person who has had a profound effect upon my life. She set me on a path in second grade that led me to success." He reached under the podium and pulled out a big cuddly brown teddy bear. "Mrs. Clayton, this is for you."

I lost it! I mean, lost it! Tears dropped from everyone.

Robert walked down the steps and walked toward me in the audience, holding out the teddy bear to me. I literally ran to meet him, crying all the way. He cried, too, and we hugged a long time while the audience clapped.

After the ceremony, Robert's dad walked up with a bouquet of yellow carnations and several cards written in Spanish. With tears in his eyes he hugged me and kept repeating, "Gracias hermosa maestra!" While I couldn't keep up with all the Spanish, his body language and his eyes spoke volumes of love.

At home I opened my beautiful cards. I read them ever so slowly and savored every word. Translated, they read: "In the most painful fights of life, when so much crookedness is around us and we cry, there is one love who will always love you, and one who will never forget you."

Signed by Robert's dad

"You showed me how to read, you showed me how to sing, you showed me how to succeed. In this day I dedicate and send one kiss from a loveable child who loves you."

Signed by Robert's mom

"Dear Mrs. Clayton, thank you for always supporting me and giving me faith in myself. I will always cherish everything you've shown me, and I'll make sure I pass on all your knowledge. Thank you so much, and I know God will keep blessing you for everything you've done."

I love you, Robert

The Barbie doll still stands atop my desk that contains the files stuffed with love notes from children I have taught. Every May I relive my last days of school memories and wish I could start all over again.

I have to be the happiest ex-teacher in the world. Thirty-one years of teaching children gave me a child's heart, and that is a heart that lasts forever!

THE ANGEL IN A BLUE AND WHITE HABIT

RENIE BURGHARDT

Be strong and courageous. Do not be terrified; do not be discouraged,

for the LORD your God will be with you wherever you go.

JOSHUA 1:9 NIV

When I began school in my new country, the United States of America, I was classified a "Displaced Person." At age fifteen, displaced also described my fragile self-esteem. Horrors of the past had taken their toll on me. My family and I had lived through World War II in Hungary, followed by four years in a refugee camp, and displaced is exactly what we were.

So there I was a mousy, shy, D.P. girl, who spoke with a thick accent and was barely acknowledged by my beautiful American peers. For beautiful is what they were to me, those girls with their ponytails and carefree, giggling ways, and I

85

longed to be just like them. But I was different; my past still haunted me.

I attended an all-girls Catholic school run by nuns, and the girls who attended came from all parts of the city we lived in, the older girls driving their cars to get there. Of course, we lived in a small rental house near the school, so I walked, and every time I entered the school, I did so with great trepidation, painfully aware of being different. I was aware that it was a great sacrifice for my grandparents, who raised me, to send me there. Money was scarce in our household, and the school had tuition, uniform, and book expenses. But I felt lucky to have been accepted, since my English was still not quite up to par.

By the time June rolled around, I had been in my new school six months. I was still shy, mousy, and barely noticed by the other girls, but despite the struggles to make my grades, I passed to the tenth grade. I was relieved. I spent that summer working part-time at a local dime store and having fun with my friends at the shores of Lake Erie.

In September of that year, it was time to don the old blue and gold jumper and white blouse and again go back to school. I entered the building with the same trepidation and dread, and although some of the girls greeted me cheerily, I had not (like many of the others) turned into a swan over the summer. But then I walked into Sister Mary Anne's sophomore English class, and soon everything changed for me.

Sister Mary Anne had the bluest eyes, a smile that lit up the classroom, and a gentle, sympathetic, understanding manner. She instantly recognized my pain and began asking me questions about my life in front of the class. She wanted my classmates to better understand why I was different from them. She explained the circumstances and gently encouraged them to put themselves in my shoes and see how they would feel in them. My mind soon concluded that God had blessed me with one of His angels for a teacher. Then the good sister gave us our first assignment of the new school term.

"I want you all to write an essay of at least four pages about something memorable that has happened to you. It will be due a week from today." When we left the classroom, for the first time at that school, I put my heart and soul into an assignment.

I wrote about being crammed, with hundreds of other immigrants, on a ship taking us to our new country. I wrote about Dave, the young American who befriended me on that ship and bought me my first Coke™. I wrote about my first sight of the Statue of Liberty, and what a thrill that was, and about being processed at Ellis Island. I wrote about how it felt to be in a new country, where the language and customs were different. And as I wrote, I realized that I loved writing.

The day after we handed in our essays, Sister Mary Anne had me read my essay aloud to the entire class. To my great surprise, my classmates applauded when I finished. Then I was sent to read it throughout the school and got the same reaction. Girls mobbed me in the hallway telling me how much they liked my essay, asking me questions, paying attention to me.

Suddenly, I was more than just a mousy, D.P. girl—I was finally becoming part of the group. Because of a caring, understanding teacher, the culture shock was broken, and to that gentle soul in the blue and white habit, I will always be grateful.

$\mathscr{A}$ GIFT OF WORDS

LYNDA BLAIR VERNALIA

For I know that through your prayers and the help

given by the Spirit of Jesus Christ, what has

happened to me will turn out for my deliverance.

PHILIPPIANS 1:19 NIV

My sophomore year my parents separated. Being so poor, they were forced to continue residing under the same roof. In our square, white, three-bedroom, Mom shared a room with her latest "boyfriend," Sam. Dad bunked with my two brothers, and I roomed with my eight-year-old half sister.

By age fifteen, I had already endured eight years of Mom and Sam constantly fighting with Dad still in the same house. The food flinging and banshee screaming were as commonplace to me as macaroni and cheese. As the youngest of Dad's four children, I was left in the midst of it all; too young to flee to college, yet just old enough to begin absorbing the implications of adultery and illegitimacy. Personal survival had become my goal, and I submerged myself in homework, as well as Cheetos™ and Coke™. I ignored my newest sibling and fabricated excuses to stay late at school and youth group functions and practiced clarinet until my jaw ached. I was living a life of crisis, and it was in the midst of this chaos that I met Mrs. Kent.

Mrs. Kent was my sophomore English teacher. I loved her. I loved her class. With a flair for the dramatic, she wore outfits thematically representing each unit we studied. She could rave about Byron's good looks, Beethoven's last years, and the weight of Odysseus' journey all in that same gentle, lilting voice. I had never met anyone before who savored language, who reveled in the sheer joy of learning, and it was very contagious. Quite by accident, I discovered that spring that Mrs. Kent and I were neighbors. She lived on the corner, only three houses down from me.

"Did you know we're neighbors?" I asked her one day after school when I had volunteered to help her with some books. "You live on the corner of my street."

"Really?" Mrs. Kent replied, a small smile lighting her bespectacled eyes. "Then maybe you would be interested in making some extra cash?" Lacking funds and eager to stay beyond the realm of my miserable habitat, I nodded.

Over the next few months, I polished silver and scrubbed windows in order to beautify Mrs. Kent's home for her only daughter's upcoming engagement party. We passed the time talking, which I did effortlessly. She directed the conversation toward life and home, mostly my home. Finally comfortable in an adult's presence, and never taught to hide the family shame, I "explained" my life at home.

"Well, my parents are separated, but neither can really afford to move out. My mom has this 'boyfriend' named Sam. He tells my little half sister, Stevie, that my dad is a bad man, and she can't talk to him. It's awful...." As I babbled, I spoke matter-of-factly, somehow distancing myself from that incredulous nightmare.

Mrs. Kent raised her eyebrows once or twice during my description of said living arrangements, but encouraged me to continue talking. A flood of emotion was being released, at last.

On one occasion, Mrs. Kent stopped me to ask if my family went to church.

"My dad takes us kids every week," I shrugged. "Mom and Sam go Saturdays."

Mrs. Kent nodded, and we returned to the polishing and cleaning.

One night in the kitchen, about two months later, Mom and Sam had a terminal fight. Trapped doing homework next to my father who was sitting at his desk in the "family" room, I witnessed the main event.

Mom had been screaming about Sam's ingratitude for the meal she was making, a pan of sautéed mushrooms flicking wildly in her hand. "You take advantage of everybody! It's not like you pay any bills around here!"

"If you don't like it, maybe I should leave," Sam sneered, flipping open yet another can of beer.

"Fine!" Mom shrieked. "Get out!" Mushrooms splattered across the carpet with her judgment, smearing a path to the front door. Horrified, I sat frozen as Sam marched to the bottom of the stairwell where Stevie stood listening.

"Well," Sam snapped at her little stricken face, "your mommy says I have to leave, so when I walk out this door you're never going to see me again." Sam then turned and left her, slamming the door behind him. That echo of finality was pierced by the desperate cries of my little sister with tiny hands pounding the wall.

The afternoon following, Dad informed me, "Your mother has filed for divorce. The house has to be sold. We're going to live with Grandma for awhile."

I was dumbstruck. *Move? Now? How could I?* I knew my future counted on good grades. Transferring schools would trash my honors points and class rank. If I didn't get scholarships, I couldn't afford college! I would never escape, as my older siblings had. I was furious with my parents, especially my mother. Her example shredded my faith.

The following Monday, I told Mrs. Kent the whole story while working at her house after school. I was almost at wit's end when she said to me, "Well, if you need to, you could stay here." Things got very quiet.

I whispered, "Do you really mean that?"

"Yes."

I went home to think about it. Later that week, when Dad picked me up from band practice, I blurted out, "Mrs. Kent said I could live with her next year if it's okay with you." The whole story came out in a flood. Since Dad was driving and could not look at me, I yammered on about class rank and scholarships and that this was what I had decided to do. He paused.

Then Dad replied, "Hon, if that's what you really want, we'll figure it out."

I collapsed beside him, *free at last.*

Mom was furious when I told her, but I did not care because I felt I was taking charge of the life she had not been looking out for. I spent the summer working at a camp to avoid the move, but kept in touch with Dad and Mrs. Kent.

That following September, I moved into Mrs. Kent's house to spend the weekdays at school, then returned to Dad on the weekends. I happily became Mrs. Kent's "fifth child."

Mrs. Kent gave so much to me. She gave me little things: shelves stocked with my favorite snacks and Chinese chicken wing takeout from dates with her husband. She gave me practical things: my very own bed in which to sleep, a desk on which to do homework, and hearty chicken and meat loaf dinners which I miss to this day. She gave me challenging things: reminders to be responsible, sighs telling me "I wish you wouldn't do that." She gave me loving things: photographs of myself in my first prom dress, a necklace from her mother, and money to spend on a class trip. The best gift she gave me, however, was a blank book and encouragement to write about my life and faith and the opportunity to work through my feelings with ink and paper.

Mrs. Kent became my very treasured life mentor and first fan. Once, she even referred to me as her "little phoenix rising from the ashes," praising my ability to overcome the many disappointments I had faced. I do not know how Mrs. K.—as I affectionately referred to her—loved me through those teenage years, but she kept taking time to talk to me as a student, as a young adult, as a Christian, and always as a writer. She gave me what my family could not, the power to express myself: in short, the gift of words.

And while I was not easy to live with, too cold, too uptight, too picky, too sad, I was now able to speak—at least on paper if not in person. There were days my books overflowed with desperation as I tried to uncover "me." Over time, however, the ranting liquefied, and I began to grasp the command of language Mrs. Kent so enjoyed. I began to explore more than just my anger; I revisited divinity and reexamined my faith. Through words, I found a hope that God was truly leading me through my challenged life, and I would emerge, not unscathed, but stronger.

Mrs. K. loved me, and I loved my new found passion. We reveled in our conversation and used our words to comfort, to heal. I never wanted to leave.

The summer before senior year, Mrs. Kent's mother became very ill, and Mrs. Kent needed to care for her. I loved Grandma Lott, but felt selfishly angry because I had to temporarily move during my senior year. Once again, vulnerability reared its claws. I was forced to rent a room from a friend's grandmother under very strict conditions, and I hated living there.

I was sad. And, I had lost my words; my ink had become dry. Mrs. Kent was now my senior Humanities teacher, but it just wasn't the same. I still loved her, but she and the words seemed so far from me.

That rift healed at Christmastime. I remember walking with friends saying, "I wonder if Mrs. K. will think of me this Christmas…." when, from around the corner, Mrs. Kent emerged with a gift bag with a giant teddy-bear head sticking out of it. As I hugged her, I knew my Mrs. K. still loved me; she had never really gone away.

I ranked eighth at graduation and received a full-tuition scholarship to college. As Mrs. Kent's protégée, I became a confident young woman and diligent writer. I will never forget her kindness or her precious, selfless investments in my life.

I have continued writing as I correspond with her over the years. She travels more often now, but our relationship is still a vibrant part of my life. Each visit, we lunch and discuss my developing manuscripts and her new endeavors. Over the years, both she and my writing have helped me return to my faith; cope with death, graduate school, marriage, and now motherhood. I know God sent me an angel in Mrs. Kent.

Mrs. Kent empowered me to give my life back to God and not be afraid to believe in those intrinsic values of love and hope. One hundred essays and one thousand poems later, I am more profoundly grateful than ever.

$\mathscr{A}$ "REAL" TEACHER, PLEASE

LANA COMSTOCK

Do not exasperate your children; instead, bring them up

in the training and instruction of the Lord.

EPHESIANS 6:4 NIV

When I took my first teaching job, I couldn't exactly call myself a teacher. I led a homeschool group, I didn't have a degree, and quite simply there wasn't anyone else to do the job.

I had been approached to teach American History to younger children. *Was it a trap? What did they possibly know that I did not?* Nervous and excited I decided to take the plunge. I tried ignoring the coming duty. I tried overplanning. I tried positive self-reinforcement…. Nothing quelled the bundle of nerves that rose up and choked me every time my mind wandered to that first day of class.

Soon, the fateful day arrived. Half relieved and half terrorized, I made my way into the classroom. *Would they laugh at me? Would I know the answers to all their questions? Would I pass out stone cold on the floor?* Only God knew. I bravely tried to trust Him.

With shaking knees I introduced myself. A student raised his hand. Here was the moment of truth. I indicated, in my most authoritative manner, that I would soon receive his question. *I was sure that like a well-oiled machine, I would come up with a brilliant answer.*

He grinned, "Ummm, in American History, will we get to study how Elvis died on the toilet?"

I paused. Tilt! Not exactly what I was expecting, but it certainly served to lighten the mood. "No, no…I guess not," I chuckled to myself. Then, I laughed. They laughed. I breathed. It was going to be okay.

A little shocking for my first question, but I went with it. I proceeded to tell my students how my mother had met Elvis at a concert just before he died. She went out to the concessions right when the show was to start. She went up to him and asked for an autograph. He lifted his sunglasses up to look at her. "You're beautiful," he said before he kissed her cheek and walked away. Not so much information about the toilet, but as close as I could come. Not only that, I had succeeded in arresting their attention. They were interested!

Weeks went by, and I began to loosen up. My true interest and excitement for a good story came through in class lessons. As a typical assignment, I often told my students to find what really interested them about a particular subject and tell me about it through a creative story.

Class lessons became my personal challenge to explore the most imaginative presentation to excite the kids. President Taft got stuck in the White House bathtub; Davy Crocket's gun had a name; Pirate treasure is still hidden in the lowlands of Galveston Island; Englishmen fought in a straight line. Whatever seemed out of the ordinary—we explored it. It proved to be a lot of fun, especially for me, but I often wondered if I was really reaching the kids.

I continually prayed and asked God to bless my efforts, to inspire my students and give them a respect and love for God's hand in history. I didn't hear much feedback from the students or their parents, but I just kept working at this newfound joy and investing my absolute best.

Finally, our school year was closing. We had a celebration to honor the work of our students throughout the year. I set up my classroom, displaying my students' projects and reports, waiting to meet and greet the parents of these kids I had grown to love.

"Mrs. C., do you have any idea how much my child loves history now?"

"Mrs. C., do you know that our daughter wants to be a history teacher since taking your class?"

Mrs. C., did you realize that my son hated creative writing until you became his teacher?"

I was so moved at their appreciation and thankful for God's mighty hand working in my small classroom. I knew that it was God who had inspired these young hearts. I couldn't help but laugh at my fumbling insecurity at the beginning of that year. Now I know that God can use anyone, because He used me.

AVOTE FOR A HERO

LANITA BRADLEY BOYD

Therefore, my beloved brethren, be steadfast,

immovable, always abounding in the work of the Lord,

knowing that your labor is not in vain in the Lord.

1 CORINTHIANS 15:58 NKJV

*A 300-word essay on why I'd vote for George Washington. Hmmm…*I thought. *That looks like a good project to follow our Revolutionary War study. And we do need an original persuasive piece for the students' portfolios. Not that my students would be likely to win the trip to Washington, D.C., but it would be fun to try.* Best of all, it didn't look like much work for me. In just a few seconds my decision was made.

We studied the life of Washington and the complete era, so I fully expected my students to reveal this background knowledge in their writings. We covered the essay structure and how to illustrate support for the points made. We wrote, revised, polished, produced, and made practice presentations in our classroom.

There were about five essays from my students that were outstanding. Four of those students being no surprise, as nearly everything they wrote was excellent, but I was especially surprised at an essay from Chris.

He had come to our school the year prior, as a fourth grader, from a school with much lower academic standards. I knew he continued to struggle, and I was delighted that he'd put so much obvious effort into this essay.

He developed the essay from the point of view of a New Englander who had served as an officer under Washington and gave excellent points signifying Washington's bravery, honesty, and love of freedom. Later I discovered that he'd chosen this point of view because of a family visit to Boston the previous summer.

I packaged the essays and mailed them off to the Mt. Vernon Ladies' Association for judging. I'd long ago learned that contest entries are best sent and forgotten, which is what we all did. Fifth grade life moved on. Months later, and to my astonishment, I received a box in the mail. The letter inside informed me that Chris Ewing had won first place in the national competition! Another of my students was a runner-up and received a beautiful t-shirt. But Chris and his parents were awarded an all-expense paid trip to our nation's capital.

His mother, Amy, later came to me with shining eyes. "Thank you so much for encouraging Chris in this contest. He really took to heart everything you said about putting yourself in that person's place.

"This is the answer to my prayers. It seemed, Chris never felt special to anyone but his dad and me, and I've been praying for an opportunity where he could catch sight of his potential. This is it! Thank you!"

I heard reports of the summer trip and the exciting flurry of sightseeing and presentations. The Ewings felt incredibly honored and appreciated. They met with our own Kentucky Senator, Wendell Ford. Their private tour of the White House was with a small group that included well-known senators. They were overwhelmed by the courtesies they received.

Chris came back to school in the fall wearing his own George Washington t-shirt—sharing pictures and stories about his trip. He was no longer the new kid, an outsider; he was our hero.

Chris has long since graduated from college as a history major with a minor in journalism and spends his summers working with underprivileged children of the South Bronx. No doubt, the opportunity from the Mt. Vernon Ladies' Association, encouragement by a tired teacher, and the fervent prayers of a dedicated mother paved the way for God's transformation in the life of a young boy—who returned that investment by devoting his best into hundreds of young, eager lives. Surely, this is God's Way.

ᶜEACHING THE WORLD

KATHRYN LAY

The Lord has announced his victory and has
revealed his righteousness to every nation!

PSALM 98:2 NLT

When my husband and I began dating, I knew that his heart was to help people from all around the world, though I never dreamed we would teach the world together.

Nine years ago, my husband, Richard, began helping two students from our local college to enlarge their English skills by meeting with them one night a week. We had worked with refugees before, helping them adjust to our country and offering our friendship. God has blessed us, as it seems people from all cultures feel comfortable talking with us.

Richard's full-time job as a teacher in the public school system kept him more than busy during the day. So, he gained the assistance of a friend to help tutor the students during the day. It wasn't long before the word quickly spread with students telling others about this man who was helping them for free.

More students came, and more help was needed. Soon classes had to be divided into two groups according to the students' skill levels and needs. Quickly this accelerated into four classes; low beginner, high beginner, intermediate, and advanced. Within six years, more than one hundred students from all around the world were coming to learn or gain a better grasp of their English reading, writing, and cultural understanding.

Before we knew it, a need for transportation for the women who were anxious to learn English began another avenue for helping our students. Every Monday and Tuesday night, two to three vanloads of women and children unloaded for classes, while still other men and women drove in their own cars.

Childcare was our next step of growth in assisting these families. Our daughter, who baby-sat small children and helped the older ones with their homework, became an integral part of this growing and changing group.

"My teacher, my teacher," a woman yelled as we walked through a department store.

A young woman who had once been a student at the school ran up to us and grabbed my husband's hand.

"Oh, teacher, it is so good to see you again. I tell you good news. Because of school, my English is better. I get job at school for small children and help the teacher." She smiled as if she were holding the President's hand. "It was you, Mr. Lay. You taught me good. I have good job. My husband happy. My children proud. I thank God for you."

She turned to me and grabbed my hand. "Thank you, too."

She hurried back to her family, who watched, then waved at us.

Through this ministry which we named "No Longer Strangers," there have been many opportunities for us and the ministry volunteers to share our faith during holiday parties and in our homes.

There have been some Monday evenings when I was tired from a day of homeschooling my daughter and would have preferred to stay home. Richard often came home exhausted and weary from a full day of teaching junior high kids. And there were times we would have rather stayed home and rested.

But, as a family, we have continued to go to our church every Monday—setting up classrooms, making copies of lessons, preparing registration test materials, making sure the other volunteer workers arrive and have the things they need to teach their students.

As teachers, we've seen our students gain better employment, feel more comfortable in meeting and making American friends, and pass their citizenship tests to become a part of this new country that they love.

We are thankful that God has brought so many students to us. Many have returned to tell of us how these classes have made their lives better.

And so it is that a new student comes into the office, and I show her to her class. Other students follow me, their clothing different from mine, their skin darker than mine, speaking broken English, broken with a heavy accent. But we hug one another, and she finds a seat. Another lesson begins, and a life is changed.

What a blessing the "No Longer Strangers" ministry has become, both to our students—and also to us.

*I*'M SO GLAD I'M IN YOUR CLASS

JOAN CLAYTON

Create in me a pure heart, God, and make my spirit right again.

PSALM 51:10 NCV

She had moved back to our school in the springtime after an extended absence of several months. Her parents had divorced.

"I'm so glad to be back in your class again," and she threw her seven-year-old arms around me.

Discovering her struggle with some of the assignments, especially in math, I took extra time during recesses to help her through the regrouping process.

She surprised me by asking if she could have extra practice papers. I was even more amazed when she brought them back the next day all perfectly done. When I displayed elation that she had mastered such difficult concepts so quickly, she enthusiastically replied: "I try to do the best I can, so I study and work hard!"

What an astonishing ideology for such a young mind, I thought. This seven-year-old had expressed a philosophy of life some adults struggle to grasp, a posture in life that would surely take her places.

Although things had obviously not been the best in this student's home, she never let it hold her back. She had a tenacious determination that became stronger each day.

Just before the Easter break I told the children to bring their colored eggs in a basket for our egg hunt. She brought her Easter eggs in a paper sack. I had kept extra baskets just in case. After the festivities she tried to give the basket back to me, but I told her it belonged to her as a gift from me. Her voice said "thank you," but her eyes spoke of a gratitude far surpassing words…eyes filled with such admiration that I had to choke back tears.

Every day as I surveyed my classroom, my heart sent up silent prayers for each of my students that they would be protected and shielded from any hurts in their young lives, especially the tender and eager heart of that one special little girl.

I'm so glad to be in the Lord's classroom. I'm grateful that His Spirit stays with me in the "recesses" of my life to help me and tutor me in the things I need to learn.

Like that special little second-grader in my class, I, too, need to study and work hard to show myself "approved unto God, a workman that needeth not to be ashamed, rightly dividing the word of truth" (2 Timothy 2:15).

When that final "bell" rings and my time in "life's school" is over I will be graduating from "Life's Classroom." Like my student, I will greet Jesus with outstretched arms, saying, "I'm so glad I'm in Your class!"

ORGIVEN

AMANDA PILGRIM

Do you despise the riches of His goodness, forbearance, and longsuffering,

not knowing that the goodness of God leads you to repentance?

ROMANS 2:4 NKJV

I tried to read his expression as anger twisted my insides. He sat stone still, glaring at me.

"How *could* you have stolen that grade book?" I demanded.

No answer.

I would have typically concocted a severe consequence to match the severity of this transgression and to make an example for the rest of the class, but I sensed God wanted me to handle this specific occurrence in a different manner.

I could see right through Jared's hollow defiance and his cold stare. I was reminded of the many times I had stumbled and made poor choices in my own life. No matter how many times I had blown it, each time God had picked me up and forgiven me. I knew that was the key to this situation. I imagined myself sitting in Jared's chair, fearful of what punishment lay in store for my misdeeds.

I slowly sat down in front of him, looking him square in the eyes and said, "I forgive you."

"What?" came his surprised reply.

"I forgive you," I said again.

"What are you going to do to me?" he asked shakily.

"Absolutely nothing. You are free to go."

He looked at me bewildered. "But I stole a grade book. Aren't you going to punish me?"

"Not this time," I said. "I am giving you an absolute pardon, wiping the slate clean, if you would like it."

I sat there quietly for a moment allowing him time to consider my words. He stared at me, and then his eyes filled with tears. "Mrs. Pilgrim, I'm so sorry. I didn't want to steal the book, but the other boys were making fun of me."

"I understand peer pressure can be very difficult to handle," I said. "We all face tough decisions in our lives. I forgive you, but I ask that you never do anything like that again, okay?"

"I promise, Mrs. Pilgrim, never."

That day I learned an invaluable lesson—to look at my students the way God looks at us—individually. I learned not to react out of emotion, but to listen to God's Spirit within me, allowing Him to guide my actions. He knows the key to unlock every heart.

HE NEW STUDENT

SUZY RYAN

God places the lonely in families;

he sets the prisoners free and gives them joy.

PSALM 68:6 NLT

It didn't take a rocket scientist to realize something was different about Ashley, my new fifth-grade PE student who had arrived a month into the school year. With limp brown hair straggling over melancholy blue eyes framed with thick glasses, she kept a downcast gaze, as if talking to my tennis shoes. Her countenance screamed, "Help me, I'm in trouble."

But trouble from what? I wondered.

I tried to keep a watchful eye on Ashley, but with 350 PE students, it was next to impossible. I had an opportunity to talk with her teacher, and found she was from a divorced family with an unusual attachment to her younger sister. When I saw her on campus, I always tried to give her extra attention.

Months later, my ten-year-old daughter, Lauren, and I were scrambling to our car after school trying to avoid being late to Lauren's swim practice. When I saw Ashley at the preschool fence talking to her little sister, I quickly gave her a hug, and to my surprise she whined as she hung on me like a toddler.

"Mom, what's wrong with that girl who wouldn't let go of you?" my daughter asked as we were driving out the school gate. I then made a mental note to talk to the principal about Ashley, which I did the next day, receiving instructions from the principal to keep her posted about any unusual behaviors.

Weeks later during PE class, Ashley was displaying a new confidence unlike her customary skittish behavior. During our flag football unit, she played the game like a normal eleven-year-old. I watched her try to get the flag from another girl, Korin, but realized that Korin had put the flag in her hair! Ashley tried to grab Korin's flag by climbing up her neck with her hands.

Korin started shrieking like a cat in water. Instantly, Ashley's confidence evaporated. Our class time was over, so I calmed Korin down and sent her and the rest of the students back to class.

I kept Ashley longer since it was my last class for the day. She stood there like a deer in headlights. I put my arm around her, trying to pull her out of her trance. "It's okay," I assured her. "You did nothing wrong."

But Ashley would have no part of it. "I'm just like her. Just like my mom. But I can't tell you. I promised I'd never tell anyone."

"You can tell me, and I won't tell anyone." Big mistake. I regretted those words as soon as they were out of my mouth. I knew I couldn't keep such a promise. By law, I was required to report abuse.

I pushed those thoughts out of my mind as Ashley's dike of emotion burst open and her words gushed out with her weeping and wiping away tears so fast that I could only make out every third syllable "She…sob…just…sob…I…sob….."

I held Ashley close, rubbing her back and stroking her hair. "She told me to never tell, but she grabs me like I grabbed Korin…she screams mean, horrible things at me…she gets me by the throat…she told me to never tell…I try to be good…." The sobbing continued.

Suddenly, it felt like someone slammed a vice grip on my head. I recalled the abuse of my own mother. Cruel words from my mom. Words that slapped me in the face, just as her hand had so many times when I was a child.

"You see why we can't tell anyone," Ashley's words snapped me back to the present. "My sister. I wouldn't want anything to happen to her."

My own forgotten memories came flooding back. "I had a baby brother. I felt I had to protect him. I carried the unfair burden of worry. *What would happen to my brother? He doesn't have a dad.* I had vowed at that point to never tell." And I never did.

Ashley's tears fell onto my hands, and I held this terrified child, fully aware of what I needed to do. I would and could help her so she could remember her fifth grade year as the turning point when she called out for help, and someone heard her. She trusted me enough to share her horror. I would not let her down.

"Ashley." I put my hands on her shoulders. "I experienced the same thing you did. My mother did everything you've told me your mother is doing to you. You're not a bad girl. You've done NOTHING wrong!" She got hysterical again, and I pulled her close to me, crying with her.

"We have to tell the principal, but I'll go with you, and she can help your mother. Your mother doesn't want to act like that. She loves you very much, but just doesn't know how to show it. I know how you feel. I have been there. I'm going to help you, Ashley. I'm going to be there for you."

We shuffled down to the office and found the principal. After Ashley told her story, the principal motioned me out of the office. I stumbled outside into the warm sun, leaned against the back of the building, and buried my face into my hands. My heart went out to Ashley. Although I knew I'd done the right thing, I was worried for her. Concerned for what her mom might do to her. Afraid for her when she went home. She had *told*.

Child Protective Services did take Ashley away, and she went to live with her father across the country. When I saw Ashley at school just before she left, she said, "I'm excited to see my dad, I'm just going to miss my sister." I hugged her one last time. We both knew that things would get better, but the road ahead would be long and sometimes hard. She'd be a new student again. She'd have to adjust to a new home. No doubt she'd miss her mother. But by fleeing her abusive situation, she had a new chance now. God would be there to comfort and renew her wounded heart. He would guide her future to see that she made it. Just as He saw that I did.

THE THINKING CHAIR

MELINDA LANCASTER

Now no chastening seems to be joyful for the present,
but painful; nevertheless, afterward it yields the peaceable
fruit of righteousness to those who have been trained by it.

HEBREWS 12:11 NKJV

Every classroom has an instigator. The four-year-old class at the local day care where I was teaching was certainly no exception. There were actually *two* little boys who often partnered in classroom crime. They might have driven several teachers to wits' end had they not been so adorable. Elaborate acts of disobedience and simple breaking of the classroom rules landed them in the "thinking chair" on nearly a daily basis.

One morning in particular they started off in unusually rare form. Our discipline system was set up in a demerit style, and we chose to call them "strikes." We had not even finished roll call before the first strike was dealt out to one of the boys. The second strike came shortly after, followed almost immediately by the third one, which of course resulted in time out in the "thinking chair." One boy giggled in delight as the head teacher doled out the punishment to the other. His laughter continued as she stomped over to the chair delivering the child by her side. No doubt in her mind, she was realizing that the early morning problems were going to make for a very long day. I suppressed a smile at the antics of the child, thinking the same thing as well.

We continued on in circle time for about a half hour with no more incidents of mischief to our great relief. I was team teaching and not yet toughened by years of experience; I always dreaded having to hand out any punishment. As we were about to break and go to the various learning centers, a voice from among the group shouted out, "What's wrong with Larry? Is he dead?" All eyes immediately went to the little spike-haired boy still sitting in the time-out area. He sat motionless in the "thinking chair" with his head tilted all the way back soundly sleeping. In an instant, the student became the teacher as a familiar verse of Scripture flashed through my mind: "Now no chastening seems to be joyful for the present, but painful; nevertheless, afterward it yields the peaceable fruit of righteousness to those who have been trained by it" (Hebrews 12:11 NKJV).

The sight of this little boy, who miraculously enough had been so quiet that he had been forgotten—taking an early morning nap, has never left my mind. The head teacher was concerned about her discipline being effective since he had fallen so fast asleep. Perhaps it did not leave a lasting impression on the child, but it did leave one on me.

I had never seen a child go willingly to the "thinking chair." And certainly not without the questions spaced at fifteen-second intervals, "How much time do I have left?" Quite often I wondered who was actually being punished…the teacher or the child. This student had been chastised, and though he did initially put up a fuss, he yielded to the discipline and, as a result, enjoyed the peace of his morning nap, waking up in a much better mood. There was no more trouble that day…no more time-outs or sitting in the "thinking chair."

So many times, I wrestle to free myself from the grip of God as He leads me to an area of time-out. He does it with my best interest in mind, to give me time to regroup and to protect me. Still all I can see is His redirection, rather than the purpose behind it. Refusing to go along peacefully, I have often resisted. No matter how elaborate my schemes of disobedience, His redirection and guidance are always for the purpose of bringing order to my life.

I am not sure what this child was thinking before he dozed off that morning, but I could not help thinking of all of the times he had spent in the "thinking chair"—and the little morning siesta that had yielded the most benefit, not just for the student but also for his teacher. The Bible says, "But God has chosen the foolish things of the world to put to shame the wise" (1 Corinthians 1:27 NKJV). That day God used the silly antics of a little spike-haired boy to teach this educator the importance of childlike submission to His loving direction.

$\mathscr{S}$HE TAUGHT MORE THAN MUSIC

NANCY GIBBS

Work hard and cheerfully at whatever you do, as though
you were working for the Lord rather than for people.

COLOSSIANS 3:23 NLT

My children's piano teacher never knew the impact, which she would make on my life. I will never forget the first time I spoke with her. She came highly recommended by a salesman at a local music store.

"If your children really want to learn, I will teach them," she said. "I am trying to slow down, but I cannot turn a pupil away if he is eager to learn. We will start next Monday."

All three children were excited about the opportunity before them. They thought Monday would never come. I bought the suggested music. After I picked them up from school, off we went for their very first lessons.

"HAVING CONFIDENCE THAT IF YOU CAN DO A LITTLE THING WELL, YOU CAN DO A BIGGER THING WELL TOO."

—*Storey*

I was shocked when I first saw the teacher. She was well into her senior years. Her fingers were bent with arthritis. She wore an exuberant smile and carried herself well, however. Her hair was pulled back into a tight bun. She had reserved three thirty-minute time slots for my children.

After I introduced my children to her, I left to pick up a few needed items at the grocery store. I didn't want to be late just in case she finished the lessons early. I returned to pick the kids up well ahead of schedule. I wondered how she could continue to play the piano with the obvious pain in her arthritic hands.

She might get tired before the ninety minutes is up, I reasoned. So I hurried back.

When I arrived back, she was in the process of teaching her second pupil. The first was doing his homework. The third was still patiently waiting. I sat down and glanced around her living room.

Everything was placed neatly on the waxed tables. Piano figurines sat on the end tables. A family Bible was positioned on her coffee table, along with several inspirational magazines. The hour and a half turned out to be more like two hours and a half. When Becky, her last student, joined us in the living room, a big smile covered her face. I felt a sense

of happiness as a result of my quiet time spent reading her
inspirational magazines.

"You have three fine children," she announced. "I think that
they will all do very well musically." I shook her hand and
affirmed that we would return the next Monday. After the four
of us got into the car, much chatter began. With smiles on each
face, my children had fallen in love with the magic of music.

When the next Monday arrived, we went back for another
afternoon filled with lessons. Again, the hour and a half slipped
into more than two hours. For weeks, the scenario was the
same. I continued to return from my shopping trips in an hour.

I began to look forward to the quiet times in her living room.
It gave me the opportunity to draw closer to God, while reading
and waiting for my children to complete their piano lessons.

The lessons were very reasonably priced in comparison to
the other piano teachers' rates. I tried to pay her extra for each
day's lessons.

"No, no," she explained. "I won't take a dime more than the
agreed upon fee."

"But you are spending a great deal of time with my children
and…."

Before I finished my sentence she chimed in. "Listen, honey. When I was a child, I took piano lessons. My teacher continuously cut my lessons short. I told the Lord that if He would allow me to learn to play the piano, I would give lessons as long as I possibly could. I promised God that I would give back to my students the extra time that my teacher took from me. That is the reason I continue to teach with these hands and the reason I teach longer than expected."

Many years have passed since the kids took piano lessons. That sweet and remarkable piano teacher has since gone to be with the Lord. Her love for music is reflected in my children's hearts, and at the same time her love for people lives in mine. In measuring her time, this remarkable teacher never failed to show her true and beautiful self. She gave more than she received while living here on earth. In the end, I am certain that this special teacher gained a much larger reward because of her generosity and sacrifice.

Today, I believe that she is playing the piano in her mansion over the hilltop, while the angels are singing along. Her hands are now healed, and her smile is more joyful as she remembers that she faithfully taught piano lessons God's Way.

$\mathscr{M}$AKING A DIFFERENCE

AMANDA PILGRIM

You are the world's light—a city on a hill, glowing

in the night for all to see. Don't hide your light!

Let it shine for all; let your good deeds glow.

MATTHEW 5:14-16 TLB

"THE GREATEST MOTIVATIONAL ACT ONE PERSON CAN DO FOR ANOTHER IS TO LISTEN."

—*Roy E. Moody*

The sun was shining, and the breeze was lightly blowing. It was a beautiful day, much too beautiful and bright to be at a funeral for a six-year-old boy.

Nicholas was without a doubt a beautiful child inside and out. His big blue eyes were always full of eagerness and wonder; his little hands always forming some special project or treat. Although he suffered from Muscular Dystrophy, Nicholas never let that hold him back from trying new things. I never thought as I looked upon this little boy full of excitement, daily searching for his favorite train to take to recess, that a year later I would be standing by his coffin consoling his mother.

After the service his mother told me what an impact I had made in Nicholas' life. I thought to myself, *I was just a young teacher trying to find my wings—what kind of difference could I have truly made in this child's life?* She told me that Nicholas loved my class and thought I was "so funny." He looked forward to seeing me and having me joke with him. I saw Nicholas fight many courageous battles at school—not being able to walk long distances without his wheelchair, needing extra assistance in the restroom, bravely learning to socialize with other children—but it never occurred to me that I would make such an impression on this child.

It is every teacher's dream to make a difference in the life of a student, to bring hope to the next generation, but to have a grieving mother with tears in her eyes look at you and thank you for inspiring her child, for that I was not prepared.

I learned to look at life differently that day. I learned that a simple pat on the back or the few moments it takes to listen to the concerns of a child can make all the difference in the world. You never know how God will use you as a blessing and a way to reach others.

ITTY-BITTY WOMAN

CANDY ARRINGTON

By this all will know that you are My disciples,

if you have love for one another.

JOHN 13:35 NKJV

Allene Bennett was an unlikely candidate for a teaching position at the alternative school. At four feet, ten inches, she hardly seemed a commanding enough presence to control and teach a classroom of problem students. However, her short stature paled to insignificance in proportion to her huge capacity to love. She had a God-given gift of discerning and meeting the unspoken needs of her students. A gift she utilized to the fullest.

Early in her teaching career, her abilities were called into question.

Gradually, her spunk and courage won her students over and gained her the title "Itty-Bitty Woman."

After several years at the alternative school, Allene encountered Polly. It wasn't long before she became aware that Polly would be her most challenging student yet. Arms folded tightly across a stained shirt, Polly marched into the classroom, headed for a seat in a far back corner of the room, and flung herself into the chair. Slouching as low as she could go without falling out of the chair, Polly began to casually draw on the desktop. Her greasy, tangled hair slanted across an unwashed face that mirrored a lifetime of hurts and unmet needs. Allene saw the pain behind the sullen expression and recognized the avoidance of eye contact as a defense mechanism. Polly was definitely going to be a challenge.

Later in the day, Allene called on Polly. "Polly, please sit up in your chair and give us the answer to number seven."

"I dunno," Polly answered without adjusting her position.

Allene let it pass and moved on to another student.

At the end of the day, Allene saw Polly slide by her desk and deposit something on one corner. After all the students had gone, Allene opened the ill-folded wad of notebook paper and read the smudged words written in cramped, all but illegible handwriting—"I HATE YOU!"

The words stabbed her heart. Slowly, she took a clean white piece of unlined paper from her bottom drawer and wrote three

words across it—"I LOVE YOU." Allene carefully folded the
paper, wrote "Polly" on the outside, and deposited it in Polly's
desk. She paused to place her hand on the desk and prayed a
silent prayer for wisdom in reaching her troubled student.

And so, a pattern was established. Each day Polly deposited
the "I hate you" note on her teacher's desk, and each day
Allene responded with an "I love you" note for Polly and a
prayer. Sometimes the teacher would include a piece of gum, a
quarter, or colorful stickers with the "I love you" notes.
Occasionally, Allene would sense detection of an all but
imperceptible softening in Polly, but always the hope was
dashed with the "I hate you" note left on her desk at the end of
the day.

Gradually, Allene began adding short encouraging words on
her notes to Polly. One day, with an accusatory voice, Polly
asked, "Why do you love me?" With this opening, Allene
began sharing tiny nuggets of truth from God's Word. However,
there was never any evidence that these seeds fell on anything
other than hard, barren ground.

As the year advanced, Polly sometimes achieved an
academic victory. Her teacher made the most of it, lavishing
her with praise and encouragement. But still the notes of
hatred continued.

On the last day of school, Polly left with the other students. Disappointment swept over Allene. What had she expected? A hug? A word of thanks? She got neither, and as she returned to her desk she was overcome with despair. For there, on the corner, was another Polly note. *Couldn't she get by just this last day without the note of hatred?*

Allene's hand trembled slightly as she reached for the note. This one looked different. Instead of the rumpled notebook paper, a pale pink piece of stationery met her touch. Carefully lettered on the outside was "Mrs. Bennett." In the bottom right corner, Polly had drawn a bright purple flower. Allene's heart beat faster as she opened the paper. Inside, written in bold magenta marker, were four simple words that melted her heart—"I LOVE YOU, TOO!"

Itty-Bitty Woman had made a great, big difference.

JONAH AND THE PRESCHOOLERS

HUGH CHAPMAN

*For I know that You are a gracious and merciful God, slow to anger
and abundant in lovingkindness, One who relents from doing harm.*

JONAH 4:2 NKJV

In the midst of the crisis, I recalled the conversation that got
me into this situation in the first place. That day, my friend had
been straightforward in his request. "We need for you to fill in
for Mrs. Weaver's Sunday school class while she recovers from
her surgery," he said. "But mostly, we need for you to keep an
eye on Josh. Can you handle that?"

I knew all about Josh...in fact, we *ALL* knew about Josh. Of
all the children in our church, he was the most consistent
behavioral problem. He was aggressive, loud, rude, and hard to
control. In fact, by now, many of the adults who had once tried
to help him had given up on Josh completely. Yet having lived

in this tiny town most of my life, I knew a little about his background, and his situation made the often annoying antics a bit easier to understand.

His father had left the family only weeks after Josh was born, and his mother had dealt with personal problems of her own. These days, in fact, he had been placed in the care of his grandmother who had developed the habit of simply dropping him off each Sunday morning when the church doors opened, then picking him up after the worship service was over.

Though Josh was the stereotypical overactive child, I anticipated little trouble, and scoffed at the absurdity of my pastor's suggestion. "Kevin, I'm 6'1" and weigh 220 pounds. I'm reasonably intelligent, and I can bench press more than 300 pounds. I think I can control a five-year-old."

Kevin snickered in a way that seemed to suggest that I might not be fully aware of what I was up against. In the face of my overconfidence, I believe that God, too, may have had a laugh...and a good one. I remained firm. "Don't worry," I assured him. "I'll have things under control."

But that initial conversation had been a week ago, and now, in the midst of turmoil, I wasn't so self-assured. Two of my assigned preschoolers had escaped earlier, and though it had taken several minutes, I finally rounded them up down the hall near the water fountain. As I held both children, one securely under each arm, they wriggled fiercely in an attempt to get away.

Now, standing in the classroom doorway, I surveyed the carnage. Half-colored cartoon drawings of "Jonah and the Whale" were scattered around the room. A little girl was sitting contentedly at the big table eating paste while two boys wrestled nearby over a broken dump truck. In another area, a kid was throwing broken crayons against a once white wall, while off in the corner, my assistant, Debi, struggled valiantly to coax a little girl out from behind the piano.

As I entered the room, a quick count revealed only seven children—someone was missing. Suddenly from the edge of the room I heard frantic pounding. My eighth child, Josh, had locked himself in the toy closet...again. I gently lowered the two escapees to the floor, then turned to latch the bottom half of the classroom's Dutch door. Having done that, I hurried to open the closet. Out stepped Josh with a frown, "You need to fix that door, Mr. Huge."

Across the room, my coworker Debi, with the help of an Oreo cookie, had finally lured the child from behind the piano. "His name is Mr. Hugh, Josh," she corrected, "not Mr.

Huge." Then, bustling past on her way to confiscate the paste, she advised, "It's time for the Bible story."

In the next moment she was cleaning paste from the little girl's hands and barking out orders to the students. "You kids settle down now—especially you, Josh, because Mr. Hugh is about to tell his story!"

I sighed, wondering how in the world I had gotten into this mess. I was a professional educator with a degree in Business Education. I should have been teaching in a high school with well-behaved, college-bound students. But with no jobs available, I had instead volunteered to help with one of the youth classes at my church. Though preschool was never what I had in mind, it was the only position they needed help with, and the job should have been a snap. But now, twenty minutes into the task, my head pounded from stress. In dismay I recalled Arnold Schwarzenegger in his famous role from "Kindergarten Cop."

In quiet turmoil, I weighed the wisdom of simply "throwing in the towel" and calling for someone more qualified. Yet I had bragged to Kevin and others about my superior teaching abilities, and now there was a matter of pride at stake. So with newfound determination, I attempted to regroup. As Debi rallied the troops, I whispered a prayer, *Okay, God, I see Your point now. Overconfidence is a bad thing. Now, please show me a way out of this mess.*

Then taking my place in front of the crowd, I began the lesson. "This is the story of Jonah," I said, in a childlike voice. "Jonah was a man whom God asked to go into Nineveh."

Immediately a joyous shout went up from someone in the crowd. It was Josh—again. "Mr. Huge is going to talk about the Nineveh Turtles!" And with that they were all up again, miniature, swashbuckling, little pizza-scarfing Ninjas doing battle with imaginary swords. I looked to Debi. "This isn't going well," I said.

She nodded in agreement. "The only thing they seem to enjoy is playtime."

It was then that I noticed again the scattered coloring pages on the floor. Picking one up, I studied the drawing; it was of Jonah in the boat during a raging storm, with a whale nearby peeking up from the water.

"Playtime," I said to myself. And suddenly an idea—one surely sent from God—began to formulate. Hurrying back to the coloring table, I slapped my palm three times against the surface. "Okay, everybody, hop up into the boat."

The little Ninjas looked to me in newfound curiosity as I patted the table again, this time with cheerful urgency. "Hurry! The boat is about to leave."

Suddenly they scampered toward the table, then stepping upon the tiny chairs each one climbed up to the top.

"Careful now," I warned. "There's no standing in the boat!"

In a moment they were all aboard, sitting cross-legged and staring attentively in anticipation of my next instruction. Hoping to avoid more trouble, I moved to the end of the table where Josh was just settling in. Then, placing my hands upon his shoulders, I said, "This is Jonah. He's the fellow I was just telling you about. Jonah is the one whom God told to go into Nineveh and preach to the people there. But do you think he wanted to go?"

The children seemed confused. Some guessed "yes," but others said "no." I took it from there. "He was just like you. Ol' Jonah wasn't sure what to do. He wanted to obey God, but he was afraid to go to Nineveh because the people there were all bad, and he was afraid they might hurt him. So instead, Jonah got on this boat headed far away from where God told him to go."

I looked to the kids. "Do you think that was a good thing?"

"Noooo," they sang in unison.

"That's right, because we should always do what God calls us to do," I said. "And when Jonah didn't do what God said, here's what happened." I lifted Josh from the table and put him onto the floor, then said, "Now Jonah, go downstairs, 'below deck' and pretend to take a nap."

The children leaned over the edge of the table and watched as Josh lay on the floor, his eyes tightly closed. Then amid the laughter of the other children, Josh began to snore. I looked to Debi who had begun to laugh, too.

Then I announced that a big storm suddenly came—I hurried over to the wall switch and turned the florescent lights quickly on and off, then excitedly I said, "In this storm there was a lot of lightning, and the people on the boat got very scared because the water started splashing up over the edges."

As if on cue, Debi rushed to the sink to run some water, then wetting her hand, she hurried back to flip water onto the faces of the children, who ducked and laughed in their reply.

"Ohhhh," I said grimly, "those people in the boat got more and more frightened, and pretty soon they grabbed up ol' Jonah and said, 'We're all going to drown! And it's all because you're not doing what God told you to do. Now, get into that water and see if the storm stops.'"

I placed my hands under Josh's arms and lifted him high into the air. Then I twirled him around the room, and as I did, I looked deeply into his expression. It was a happy, laughing, loving face, and it made me consider all the horrible things I had heard about him. He was just a child. One who had been abandoned by his father and neglected by his mother. There was no evil, nor was there hatefulness. He was just a boy trying to make his way in a world he didn't understand. He just needed love and understanding. I spun him in a circle, once, twice, then three times until finally I placed him softly near a second table, which was covered with a cloth.

"When Jonah left the boat, the storm finally stopped," I told them. "But God didn't want Jonah to drown, so He caused a big fish to swim up and swallow him!" I raised a portion of the tablecloth and put it over Josh's head, and he quickly scooted further beneath the table…into the belly of that huge fish. I then peeked under the cloth and into Josh's laughing face. He shrugged happily, sighed, and then whispered in a tiny voice, "I love you, Mis-ter. Huge."

And suddenly, it became clear to me why God had put me here in this place at this time. Josh needed someone to understand him, someone who could throw a football to him, and who could lift him high into the air. He needed someone to be a buddy to him. His mother had probably tried, and perhaps his grandmother, too, and the little ladies from his Sunday school class, as well. But today I finally understood—Josh needed something more. I looked into his eyes and choked back a feeling of pride. And then—in the way that a father might tell his own son—I whispered my reply, "And I love you, Josh."

For a minute there was a mutual silence, as Josh and I looked to one another in our newfound friendship. Then, backing away from beneath the table, I turned to the other children, who seemed to wait excitedly for the conclusion of the story. But in my own heart, the important lesson was clear. It's not up to us to choose what tasks we undertake for God. Rather, we must learn to trust Him. And like Jonah before us, we must learn never to question what we're told.

I turned to the others in an attempt to put closure to the lesson, as quietly I asked, "Boys and girls, do you know what happened next?"

Yet before anyone could answer, to my dismay, Josh leapt from beneath the tablecloth, and with arms raised in triumph he shouted, "THE WHALE PUKED ME BACK!"

I looked to Debi who cringed in slight embarrassment. "I…guess I told them a little about the story—when you were chasing those kids down the hall."

I sighed. Nobody said teaching was going to be easy.

IN MOMENTS LIKE THESE

EILEEN ZYGARLICKE

For God is not unfair. He will not forget how hard you have

worked for him and how you have shown your love to him

by caring for other Christians, as you still do.

HEBREWS 6:10 NLT

"This is it! If this doesn't get them talking, nothing will," I said to myself as I cut out a news story for a current events discussion in my government class. The next day, however, was another disappointment. I finally felt I was ready to meet the enemy, better known as my students. However, instead of generating the hoped-for discussion, my students were retreating deep into the recesses of their minds, leaving behind bored, vacant stares. In frustration, I turned a potential interactive discussion into a writing assignment. Those vacant, glazed looks quickly turned into hostile glares.

"BELIEVE, WHEN YOU ARE MOST UNHAPPY, THAT THERE IS SOMETHING FOR YOU TO DO IN THE WORLD. SO LONG AS YOU CAN SWEETEN ANOTHER'S PAIN, LIFE IS NOT IN VAIN."

—*Helen Keller*

After the students left, I sat in my classroom and literally cried out to God. *Why couldn't I get through to these students? How could I get my class to think? Better yet, how could I get them to respond?* I prayed that day for what seemed to be an endless time and was shocked at the response that came to me. It was the same response I had gotten from my students— silence. *God, where are You, and what am I doing wrong?*

As I left school that day, my mind continued to churn, dwelling on all the possible avenues of attack I could take in fighting this war on apathy which had broken out in my classroom in September and was continuing on six months later. Something had to work. I just had to find out what.

I tried the next day and the day after that and the day after that until six months turned into nine months and the year was drawing to a close. I had won and lost some battles, occasionally engaging my students briefly in some form of dialogue, but looking back over the months, I could say with conviction and frustration, it seemed I had lost the war.

The last day of class was spent discussing plans for college and career choices among the students. Most were headed to the local university to continue their education. One of my students, Lisa, had always been a favorite of mine. She had a quick mind and a gentle spirit, and seemed open to following the Lord for her future. When Lisa's turn came to tell what she was going to do in the fall, she said that she wanted to pursue a career in law. I encouraged the students to consider their career choices with much thought, telling them how important it was for them to follow the divine direction for their lives with care.

The bell rang, and I watched my students hurriedly stumble to the door, freeing themselves from the bondage of school and specifically my government class. My heart was heavy. I felt as though I had failed to obtain any of the goals I had set for myself. I had put more time and effort into this class than any of my other classes, yet not one of the students seemed to comprehend it.

A whole school year was gone, and I had nothing to show from it. I was feeling a bit sorry for myself, wondering if I was still doing what God wanted me to do. I felt as though I had failed to equip these young adults that God had entrusted to me. Were they ready for the real world? Could they discern between truth and opinion when sitting in a college class? As a Christian educator, I wanted them to live a godly life and follow the direction God had for their lives, even if it meant a change of career course for them. Despite the failure that surrounded me, I knew I had done my best. Now I had to trust God.

Three more government classes passed, and I had almost forgotten the feelings of frustration that one group of students evoked in me. Then I ran into Lisa at a store where she was working as a sales clerk. Surprised to see her, I asked how she was doing. Her face was radiant as she explained how she had thought about what I had said that last day in government class about seeking the purpose and direction for our lives when choosing a career. Lisa went on to say how she had always wanted to be a lawyer and had just assumed God wanted it too. Then, as she began to pray about it, a new desire grew within her. A desire she acted upon. Lisa had decided to pursue a degree in secondary education. She wanted to become a social studies teacher.

I was stunned by this revelation. Then I laughingly asked her why she would ever want to be a teacher. As I looked at her, though, Lisa wasn't laughing. She had a soft smile upon her lips as she told me that she wanted to impact young people the same way I had impacted and influenced her and others in her class.

She told me her friends from high school still talked about that government class and all they learned and all the fun they had had. According to her, I had instilled in her a love for history, politics, and teens. Lisa nodded her head, smiling as she told me she thought it would be a privilege to serve God just like I had—by being a teacher.

A wave of shock enveloped me. I mumbled something unintelligible as Lisa moved on to wait on a customer. All of that whining and crying out to God and self-pitying…what had it all been for? I realized at that point how little I had trusted God in bringing home to the students the ideas I wanted to convey. I had sold God short and also my students, and I felt terrible. I made my way out to my car, abandoning my shopping venture. As I sat in the parking lot, I repented for my lack of faith and trust in Him. Slowly my tears turned to joy. I had reached them. Those students who had sat through all of my classes, stony-faced, had really been absorbing what I had said. In moments like these, all of the pain and preparation for that class had been worth it. It really was a privilege serving God by being a teacher.

THE "HOPELESS CLASS"

WILLIE BELL

(as told to Muriel Larson)

And they that know thy name will put their trust in thee:

for thou, LORD, hast not forsaken them that seek thee.

PSALM 9:10

The doctor rested his glasses against his chin and looked seriously at me. "You have all the symptoms of battle fatigue," he said. "Frankly, I don't see how you can cope with another school year."

Unbidden tears filled in my eyes.

"You must be under a lot of pressure," the doctor remarked.

"Yes, I am," I sobbed, telling of three hospitalized family members. "But if I have to give up teaching, it would seem like a death sentence!"

"Well, then," the doctor conceded, "maybe you *would* be better off teaching."

When I got my roll for the coming year, however, I wondered. Another teacher had remarked, "If I get that one group coming up from fourth grade, I think I'll resign!" And I had been assigned that "hopeless class." Twenty-six of the twenty-eight students came from broken homes, and many were known troublemakers.

Lord, I prayed, *I would appreciate You giving me an extra portion of strength this year. What these children need is a teacher who will understand them and be able to get through to them. Help me become that kind of teacher!* I bowed in prayer for each child listed.

Then I looked at my upcoming class and program with new eyes. I knew that with these special children I would have to abandon the traditional approach. As new ideas came and as I recalled things that had worked in the past, I felt God's guiding hand near.

After rearranging the room so that I could see each face, I made a "cozy corner" for "fireside chats" and a "communications center." I planned a bulletin board to feature a special student each week.

"Children," I greeted them the first day, "I have saved many things for you to help me do. I have made backgrounds for bulletin boards, but I want you to make up the boards yourselves. How many of you feel you can do it?" Every hand shot up.

Later I explained the communication center. "You can write me little notes and put them in the mailbox," I said. "Never go home with a burden on your heart. And I will try to find time to answer all your notes."

During the days that followed my students wrote me many notes, helping me to understand them and their circumstances better. This was an excellent opportunity to encourage, as well as a great exercise for reinforcing creative writing, sentence structure, and paragraphing—because the children were motivated to write. They also loved our "fireside chats" in the cozy corner. I had no discipline problems!

BUILDING SELF-ESTEEM

I knew one of the big problems that troubled these children was low self-esteem. I tackled this problem by having a bulletin board, which regularly featured "The Student of the Week" with a photograph. This recognition was given to a child who was making good progress, was smiling the most, and was one who lifted others up. This approach worked wonders in the class.

Sheila had displayed many problems the year before, often getting into fights. During the second week of school she declared, "I feel really good about myself! That girl out in the hall wanted to fight, and I just told her I wasn't in a fighting mood. I didn't even hit her back!"

"Sheila, this makes me very proud of you!" I exclaimed. "You are ten feet tall to me. Now I know that other person admires you, too."

During our fireside chats on Fridays I would say about a child who looked discouraged that day, "I know something good about Ricky. He had a nice, big smile yesterday." Then the children would join in, naming one good thing after another about the boy. It would be tape recorded, and Ricky would take the tape and a recorder home and play it for his mother.

Another avenue, which became very effective, was allowing the children to air their troubles anonymously through writing to "Dear Abby," using the fictitious names of "Chip" and "Meg." And through counseling the children, and later their parents, I was able to alleviate several troubled situations.

The children learned reading and writing through letter, story, and playwriting. They tackled math through a buddy system, where a brighter student helped another until he understood the principle. At the end of the school year my children had made more progress in math than any of the other fifth grade classes.

My class also had one of the best attendance records in the school. The principal no longer had my students frequenting his office.

I also started parent education, inviting them to observe. During personal conferences with parents, I listened a lot and tried not to preach.

As various supervisors of the county school system learned what was going on, they began to bring in groups of twenty-five to thirty teachers to observe my class. I soon started conducting workshops for other teachers.

That spring, thanks to God's guidance, I was chosen as the outstanding educator in adult education for the State of South Carolina. What an honor that was for me. But truly the award nearest to my heart was the plaque presented to me by the children and parents of my fifth grade class that read *"Teacher of the Year."*

UNDERWATER BASKET WEAVING

DARLA SATTERFIELD DAVIS

In fact, in his public teaching he taught only

with parables, but afterward when he was alone with

his disciples, he explained the meaning to them.

MARK 4:34 NLT

In college I had an instructor by the name of Dr. Fran
Mosley. I have said many times that Dr. Mosley could teach
"Underwater Basket Weaving" and make it pertinent and vital
to life. The point being that no matter what subject she taught
she incorporated important life lessons and essential learning
into the course. I took several classes with her, and though she
was known to be tough and give generous amounts of work,
her classes were always overflowing with students.

I watched her teach "American History" and "Legal,
Philosophical, and Ethical Foundations of Teaching" with the

"LIVES OF
GREAT MEN
ALL REMIND
US WE CAN
MAKE OUR
LIVES
SUBLIME;
AND,
DEPARTING,
LEAVE
BEHIND US,
FOOTPRINTS
ON THE
SANDS OF
TIME."

—*Henry Wadsworth
Longfellow*

same spellbinding finesse. I wanted more than anything to be the caliber of teacher I saw in her, so I began to watch her teaching style in addition to learning her subjects.

She had a winning attitude about her that was contagious. She began our classes by informing us that we each had an "A" in her class already so the pressure was off. She followed that statement by smiling and informing us that our job was to "keep" that A status during the course. She sprinkled cartoons and jokes throughout her difficult tests that eased the tension and helped us do better. She made eye contact with each of us and acknowledged us as we entered and left her class. She made teaching and learning personal and enjoyable with numerous examples and thoughts to ponder.

One common thread that wound its way through all her courses was the importance of what we were learning as it related to life. All of her classes became meaningful because she brought them to the practical side of everyday living and teaching.

In my senior year I finally put my finger on what made Dr. Mosley's teaching style so different and effective. She had done for us what Jesus had so often done for His disciples. She had taken everyday lessons and showed the deeper meaning and how to apply what she was teaching. She loved us. She had high expectations, and helped us achieve the desired outcomes.

When I think back about Dr. Mosley and her great teaching methods I do want to strive to be more like her—because she was striving to be more like Jesus.

 A SHINING EXAMPLE

AMANDA PILGRIM

Set an example for the believers in speech,

in life, in love, in faith and in purity.

1 TIMOTHY 4:12 NIV

She never won any awards or was highly acclaimed in her field, but Coach Harrison was my hero. She was strong, supportive, and she believed in me.

I began playing basketball in the seventh grade. I was awkward and had no idea what to do on the court, but Coach Harrison was there. She taught me the rules, the basics, and a love for athletics.

She was there urging me on when I wanted to give up and throw in the towel. She was there to support me when I was angry and hurt. She was there to push me to the next level when I refused to push myself.

Coach Harrison was more than just a coach—she was an example of what a teacher is supposed to be, someone to help you when you fall down, to challenge and encourage you through to the next finishing line, someone you can look up to and respect.

She never allowed us to play dirty, take cheap shots, or bad-mouth our opposing teams. To her, it really was about "how" you played the game. Coach Harrison taught me many things over the years, but the most important ones were how to be a respectable person, play fair, play hard, and give it 110 percent. She instilled in me so much more than a desire to play hard and with passion in the game, but also to play hard and with passion in life.

I think of Coach Cheri Harrison as I coach my own basketball teams. I try to inspire my teams as she inspired me. As I challenge my teams to press on in life to become better individuals, I often think of her influence and investments into my own life.

I thank God for teachers like Coach Harrison, who showed me what it was to be a better person.

IT'S GOING TO BE A GREAT YEAR

JANET LYNN MITCHELL

And you should follow my example, just as I follow Christ's.

1 C O R I N T H I A N S 11:1 NLT

Following tradition, the night before a new school year began, Marty, my husband, and I took each of our children aside and prayed with them committing the school year to God. As we turned to our son, Jason, my husband prayed, *Lord, I ask that You would bless Jason and his eighth grade year. Help him to learn all You have for him, and may You provide for each of his needs. Amen.*

That's it? I thought as my husband finished his prayer. *Jason's entering the eighth grade in a public school! Shouldn't you pray that he makes good friends, has great teachers, and stays on the straight and narrow?*

"Son, it's going to be a great year," Marty concluded as Jason left the room. The first week of school went by. Jason seemed to be happy with his schedule, teachers, and classes, yet he also had a request.

"Mom, Mr. Reid has asked me to be his teacher's assistant for the sixth-period class. I really want to, Mom. Can I?"

"What class do you have sixth period?"

"I have Spanish. I can take Spanish my freshman year of high school. Won't you sign this permission slip?"

I took the permission slip and set it on the counter. Jason knew that I wanted to run this grand idea past his father. As I prepared dinner, I thought about Mr. Reid and what kind of man he was. "He's cool and understands kids!" I could hear Jason saying. Even though Mr. Reid was one of the youngest teachers at the school, he had gained the admiration of all—the students, staff, and parents. I also knew that Mr. Reid's activities outside of school consisted of working with a youth group at a local church. In a conversation Jason had with Mr. Reid the past year, Jason had told him that we were believers.

That night Marty and I sat down to discuss Jason's future possibilities of becoming a teacher's assistant. We ran through the list of jobs Jason told us he would be performing. All of them seemed to be comprised of busy work, and we were certain that it would help Mr. Reid. Yet, our decision to allow Jason to become Mr. Reid's teacher assistant was not based solely on how Jason could help Mr. Reid, but what Jason could receive from Mr. Reid. We were willing to allow our son to delay his Spanish class in order for Mr. Reid to be a mentor to our son.

Jason's eighth grade year was truly a year to remember. Jason grew in wisdom and stature. He had a Godly man, at a public school, who was willing to take the time to make a positive imprint upon his life. I don't think that any other teacher has had a greater influence on our son than Mr. Reid.

Looking back, I remember Marty's prayer at the beginning of the school year. *Lord, I ask that You would bless Jason and his eight grade year. Help him to learn all You have for him, and may You provide for each of his needs.* God did bless our son in ways we never expected—through the life of a wonderful, Godly man named Mr. Reid.

A BABY SHOWER FOR MIZ JONES

LOUISE TUCKER JONES

What I want is for you to receive a well-earned

reward because of your kindness.

PHILIPPIANS 4:17 NLT

I was barely twenty-two years old, straight out of college and three months pregnant with my first child when I began my teaching career. On top of this I was living alone for the first time in my life while my husband was stationed in another city for six weeks on his tour of duty in the Army.

It was a lot to handle, and the school system didn't make it any easier when they assigned me to one of the roughest junior high schools in the city where I taught Spanish and English. Vandalism was rampant, and there were often knife fights in the courtyard.

"IT IS ONE OF THE MOST BEAUTIFUL COMPENSA-TIONS OF LIFE THAT NO MAN CAN SINCERELY TRY TO HELP ANOTHER WITHOUT HELPING HIMSELF."
—*Ralph Waldo Emerson*

Never being raised with prejudice, the large minority population didn't bother me, but the lack of respect did. Students often caused chaos in the classroom and made derogatory remarks or racial slurs. To my surprise, the girls were the worst offenders. Almost every day you could find a young lady sitting in a desk outside the door of my classroom because of disruptive behavior.

The boys knew a greater punishment awaited them if they caused problems. The teacher across the hall—a tall, heavy, intimidating man—came into my room the first day of school and introduced himself. He said, "If any of these boys cause you trouble, just send them to me, and I'll take care of them." I did, and he did! If only someone could handle these girls!

Each day, I would be physically and mentally exhausted by the time I got home to our little duplex. At night, I prepared lesson plans, sewed maternity clothes since I could not afford to buy them, and would drag myself to bed before ten o'clock. The next morning I would get up early, sit on the side of my bed for a nauseous moment, then run to the bathroom and throw up. My daily routine. Then I would face my students, trying desperately to reach them and meet their needs.

Many seemed to be responding, especially in my Spanish classes where I let them act out real life situations such as ordering meals at a restaurant. They threw all the drama they could into their parts. I even planned an evening party for the students, hoping to meet their parents, but few attended.

About six weeks into the school term, I could wait no longer to switch my wardrobe. Maternity clothes were a must, and the girls noticed immediately. There were whispers and giggles, then finally an outright question during class. "Miz Jones, are you gonna have a baby?" I smiled and answered, "I certainly am."

What difference that made I'm not sure, but my students began acting a little nicer. Even the boys were more polite, and the girls started hanging around after class to ask me questions. Now they knew why I had sometimes gone flying out of the classroom and running down the hallway. They seemed genuinely concerned to find that I was throwing up in the bathroom due to my pregnancy.

Students began taking it upon themselves to chastise other students who caused me problems. No one was to bother Miz Jones because she was going to have a baby. Their tough hearts seemed to melt a little more each day.

When the semester ended, so did my teaching career for that year with only two months before the baby's due date. On my last day of school, the big, burly teacher from across the hall detained me outside my classroom. This was unusual, and I suddenly became suspicious. *Had the kids done something awful? Why was he keeping me from entering my classroom?*

Finally, I opened the door to a chorus of "Surprise!"

My students were ecstatic. They had a few wrapped presents on my desk and some treats that the principal approved when they told him they wanted to give me a surprise baby shower. We spent time laughing and talking as the kids congregated around my desk to watch me open the small gifts of baby bibs, pacifiers, and such. There were cards with sweet sentiments, and no one wanted me to leave. "We'll never know if you had a girl or a boy." One student remarked, "We want to see the baby." I promised them I would bring the baby to see them sometime the next semester.

True to my word I took my little baby boy up to the school one spring afternoon and disrupted the class of students who had given me the baby shower. The new teacher graciously allowed the students to "ooh" and "ah" over my precious bundle, and the students seemed genuinely touched that I had kept my promise.

My next teaching assignment took me to a high school on the other side of town, so I never saw my junior high students again, though I thought of them often through the years. No, I didn't wonder if they could speak Spanish fluently or get their commas just right in English. I did, however, wonder if they remembered a very pregnant teacher who had loved them genuinely and who had hoped to have made a difference in their lives.

I also wondered if they had any idea what an impact they made on my own life. You see, after thirty-five years, I still have those "baby shower" cards scribbled with seventh grade sentiments. And my baby boy? Well, he grew up and became a teacher, too!

ＪUST AS SURE AS THE WIND BLOWS

DIANE H. PITTS

The Lord will open the heavens, the storehouse

of his bounty, to send rain on your land in season

and to bless all the work of your hands.

DEUTERONOMY 28:12 NIV

"NO WINTER
LASTS
FOREVER;
NO SPRING
SKIPS ITS
TURN."

—Hal Borland

Purple black clouds hung suspended in clusters above the earth, threatening showers yet unleashing a breeze to lighten a balmy Saturday. The afternoon slowed when my husband and two older boys rambled off for a work project, leaving six-year-old John Will and me at home. Wanting to stall the storm and capture the moment, I herded John into the field for berry picking. Maybe some uninterrupted time together would relieve my heartache over last week's turmoil in John's kindergarten.

I blocked out the worries and thought back to previous years when we had cleared some of the wooded area now obscured by overgrowth—brambles, high grass, and a new generation of trees. We couldn't see berries, but since the older boys had reported some patches, John and I decided to go on the hunt. Off we plunged, looking for remnants of the old path that might allow a safer journey through briers. We proceeded on our quest, looking but not yet finding.

"Mommy, I know those berries are here! The brothers told me. We'll find them. Just keep looking with me." His eyes shone in anticipation of the discovery. I knew the possible disappointment of being empty-handed, but I chose to keep searching; how could I dampen his exuberance?

We traveled on, the wind occasionally whipping hair into our faces, briers scraping hands and legs, and eyes aching to see purple berries. John's shout pierced the steady crunch, crunch of our feet.

"Mommy, berries! Look!" John dropped my hand and plunged ahead. "Can we get these red ones?" His face glistened with sweat and the glory of the prize.

I shook my head slowly and gently said, "No, John. Those aren't ready. They have to be purplish blue—like this one." I saw an edible berry guarded by a hundred briers.

Carefully, I secured it but not without cost to my hand. John immediately turned his attention to the small wound. With difficulty, I got him back on the search for more berries.

In a few minutes, we hit the jackpot, only the harvest was red. Everywhere, red! Because of past berry-picking experience, I knew that soon red would turn to purple. Before long, they would be ready. Just not now. Although we continued to scour the area, the yield remained small.

"John, keep going," I encouraged. His eagerness flagged even though I let him pick any suitable berries that appeared. He wanted to turn back. Finally, the ultimate question surfaced.

"Mommy, will they ever get ripe? When?" His lips quivered. "How long will I have to wait?" He explored my face for the response.

As I gazed into the face of a little boy with a thousand questions, I saw a bright mind and a love of learning as well as a volatile, creative personality. I considered the years ahead— the possibilities as well as the pain. The kindergarten chaos fought its way to the surface of my thoughts, but in the midst of all the contemplation someone else stood out—his teacher, Mrs. Minnie Demetropilis, affectionately known as Mrs. Dee.

She was the kindergarten teacher God provided to love John on the first leg of his educational journey. She believed in what God could do in him.

Mrs. Dee started ABC Kindergarten in our close-knit community; she would have retired this year but stayed another year, and one of the reasons was John. A longtime friend of the family, we had asked her to pour her life into one more student who needed her special touch. Despite her weariness and personal tragedies, she agreed to teach one more kindergarten class—a class that included our son.

She was the first to greet John when he entered K5. Mrs. Dee guided him through the difficult maze of phonics, whispering encouragement when things grew hard and the path was not readily apparent. She provided discipline when he became combative or answered in defiance—his way of wanting off the trail. She saw what others had difficulty seeing; it takes time to mold a character, and the journey becomes long and tedious. However, Mrs. Dee believed the fruit would appear in John's life, just as sure as the wind blows, and the laws of harvest persist. She had encouraged us to persevere.

"He's going to make it. The fruit of our labor is going to come! Know it."

My rambling thoughts dissipated like morning mist, and I was brought back to the perplexed blue eyes before me.

"Will they ever be ripe, Mommy?" he repeated.

I studied the face of the future, remembered Mrs. Dee, and replied with certainty, "John, these red berries mean that the purple fruit is coming; just as sure as the wind blows, just as sure as God makes the sun shine, the berries will come!"

And so will the fruit of your life, my son. Know it!

John grabbed my hand, and we turned toward home with the few trophies we had gleaned. But there will be another day. Another day of trophies. Just as sure as the wind blows, the berries will be purple. I just know it!

THE SCIENCE FAIR

ANNETTEE BUDZBAN

The steps of a good man are ordered by

the Lord: and he delighteth in his way.

PSALM 37:23

"THE GREAT
MAJORITY
OF MEN ARE
BUNDLES OF
BEGINNINGS."

—Emerson

When I was in school, my friend and I were signed up for a "special project" by our teacher for the science fair. We were eager to please. However, we wondered—*what on earth was this project we were signed up for?* The Reproductive System—*What is that?*

Our teacher went on to explain that this project entailed molding out of clay, models of the birth cycle, from conception through nine months. *You have got to be kidding!* I thought. *I am no sculptor!* Neither was my friend. We were bewildered as to how we would make this come about. But, our teacher reassured us that she had every intent on helping us with this task.

I was given a science book and started reading immediately. Before long, I was actually fascinated with this process! The process of life was an amazing discovery. Now, how could we put these pictures into form?

With our teacher's assistance, we decided to use a large poster board as our display background; this aided in deciding what size to make each clay model. Next, we would need to mold one model for each month of gestation. That meant a total of nine models of an egg cell and each stage it was in. We would have to keep each model fairly small.

We worked tediously as we continued to study the process and mold each figure. Life was now taking form before our very eyes. It was actually turning out very well.

With each clay model positioned on a poster board, it was my first depiction of how a baby is formed. Each one started to look real to me. How we managed this still amazes me to this day!

The day of the fair arrived. The whole gymnasium was filled with science projects. Our classmates started to come by and eye our display and ask us many questions. We were now finding ourselves teaching others what we had learned.

People were hanging around our display. You should have seen the crowd! More and more of our classmates were flocking to our project. There was no competition. They no longer eyed the erupting volcanoes, or the mysteries of combustion! They, too, were intrigued with the formation of life.

We won first place. This honor won us the privilege of having our picture in the newspaper. What a thrill!

I never forgot my fascination with life and birth…I guess that is why I went on to become a registered nurse and worked with expectant mothers giving birth. I also loved teaching about prenatal life, and I became a Natural Childbirth Instructor. I will be forever grateful to my teacher for offering me the opportunity to participate in this project for our science fair, which molded my life.

The Bible teaches us that our steps are ordered by the Lord. I look back in awe, as I see how He ordered my steps that day, when my teacher approached me. I have often wondered if simply being willing to fulfill that task is what made my life take form.

It is in these small moments of absolute, innocent trust and surrender that we allow God to move in our lives. What is God asking you to do?

A LASTING LEGACY

ESTHER M. BAILEY

*I urge you, dear brothers and sisters, to respect them fully
and others like them who serve with such real devotion.*

1 C O R I N T H I A N S 1 6 : 1 5 - 1 6 NLT

"ONE GOOD
TEACHER IN
A LIFETIME
MAY
SOMETIMES
CHANGE A
DELINQUENT
INTO
A SOLID
CITIZEN."
—*Philip Wylie*

It was a beautiful summer day, and the streets of the small
town of Oakes, North Dakota, found visitors bustling
everywhere. Like many others, my husband, Ray, and I had
come for the Centennial Celebration of his hometown. It was
my first trip there as his new wife.

Almost as soon as we arrived, someone stopped my husband.
"You're Ma Bailey's son, aren't you?" the stranger asked.

Always pleased to acknowledge his mother, Ray said, "Yes."

In response the stranger enthusiastically stated, "She was
my favorite teacher. I learned more about grammar during the
year she taught than from all the rest of my schooling put
together—even college."

The typical comment was the first of many yet to come during the three-day event. No matter where we went—from the restaurant, to the ball park, to church—someone had something good to say about the teacher, affectionately known as Ma Bailey.

It had been thirty-four years since my husband's graduation from Oakes High School. As we toured the facility, our escort's eyes twinkled as she led us to the "wall of fame." After seventeen years, Ma Bailey's picture still hung beside other prominent educators.

Unfortunately, I never had the opportunity to meet my mother-in-law, but I felt that I already knew her because I had heard so much about her from my husband. Anytime the subject of Heaven comes up at our house, Ray usually says, "I can't wait to introduce you to my mother." And I genuinely look forward to that meeting.

Life had not always been easy for the woman who raised two sons alone. After a divorce, she completed the academic requirements to earn a teaching certificate as a means of supporting her family. At the same time she was developing life skills and building character in her students.

When her sons left home, Ms. Bailey devoted all her energy to her career. Preparing young people for successful living became her primary objective.

To the very end she remained faithful to her cause. Although she wasn't feeling well one day, she went to school and taught until noon. She went home in the afternoon and passed away only a few hours later.

Among my husband's cherished possessions is a notebook put together by former students of his mother. The well-composed tributes to a beloved teacher testify to the value of her efforts and investments.

It's one thing to hear good things about someone at a funeral or shortly after. Keeping the legacy alive for nearly forty years indicates the profound influence on the lives of others.

The many words of praise spoken about Ms. Bailey during that Centennial Celebration proved that her place in academic history is secure.

Memory of my exposure to people who loved my mother-in-law and appreciated her teaching triggers thoughts of my sixth-grade teacher who helped me lay the foundation for what has brought me my greatest satisfaction in life.

The life-changing experience for me began in English class near the end of the year. A paragraph under consideration contained a sentence similar to this: The bouquet of roses add an elegant touch to the table.

"What's the problem with that sentence?" Miss Jenkins asked the class. We all remained mute.

In an effort to help us figure out the answer for ourselves, the teacher asked, "What is the subject of the sentence?" When no one volunteered to answer, Miss Jenkins called on me.

My guess was wrong. No one else knew either. We didn't know the difference between a subject and a predicate or a noun and an adjective.

Dismayed, Miss Jenkins said, "You should know all this by now. Nothing you ever learn will be more important than grammar. Good language skills may mean the difference between a good job and a mediocre one. With the right words you can persuade others to consider your way of thinking. No matter what you do in life, you need the ability to express yourself properly."

At that time I didn't know what I wanted to do with my life, but I was certainly convinced that my future depended upon how well I knew the English language. For me, that day began a lifelong quest for learning the rudiments of communication.

For the rest of the term, Miss Jenkins shortened our lessons in history, geography, science, and even math to drill us on parts of speech, punctuation, tenses, and the many other facets of correct grammatical usage.

We learned to diagram sentences and apply the rules to everyday conversation. By the end of that year I was ready to answer the questions on the final exam, and my love for putting words together has served me well—through the rest of my schooling and throughout a business career.

Eventually, I became a published author with an approximate thousand articles or stories and several books to my credit. I would like to hope that my writing has made a difference in the lives of my readers. If my words have conveyed God's love to someone who is hurting or offered hope to one in despair, my sixth-grade teacher deserves some of the credit.

As I recall the tributes paid to Ma Bailey I am reminded of my own negligence. I lost track of Miss Jenkins and never went back to thank her for inspiring me to build a foundation on which my life's work rests. I wish I had used the best of my communication skills to express my appreciation to the woman who opened the door of the literary world for me.

Perhaps I can yet make amends for my oversight. The best way I know to pay a debt of gratitude to educators of the past is to extend a tribute to all teachers who are currently preparing students to make the world a better place in which to live. I'm sure my beloved teacher and my mother-in-law would both be pleased to know that their legacies continue on through dedicated teachers of today.

SCRAMBLED CHRISTMAS

DARLA SATTERFIELD DAVIS

These commandments that I give you today are to be upon your hearts.

Impress them on your children. Talk about them when you sit at home and

when you walk along the road, when you lie down and when you get up.

DEUTERONOMY 6:6-7 NIV

"Deck the Halls with Bowls of Jelly!" Timmy skipped into the art room singing at the top of his lungs. "Good morning, Timmy," I said to the youngest of my first grade artists. "Please take your seat and save the singing for the music room—or your shower," I said with a wink. The students all giggled and eventually found their seats.

"Today we are going to take a look at our artwork from yesterday titled 'What is Christmas?' Timmy, since you are still standing and so excited, will you begin, please? Here is your paper; please tell us about your work," I said wondering if even

Timmy himself could decipher the explosion of color and figures scattered around his page.

And so began the most amazing Christmas story ever told! "Well, look here," Timmy began with enthusiasm. "This is where a big star was fallin' on some shepherds, and the angels were busy singing, so the guys on the camels had to come and save them." The class looked confused, but Timmy gave them no time to comment or protest. "An' over here is where Santa Claus came down the 'chimbly' and brought the baby Jesus to Mary who wanted one for Christmas real bad." Timmy looked up to make sure everyone could see his jumbled figures and bright splotches. "Mary cooked Joseph's goose for Christmas, and they invited the Indians for dinner." My eyebrows shot up, but sheer curiosity kept me silent.

Timmy continued across the page pointing out the details as he went along. "The king didn't like the baby, so they put a tree in the window for cover, and decorated it with stuff from Wal-Mart. And the star that fell went on the top of the tree! Rudolph and the red-nosed reindeers played some games and watched the baby Jesus, and a cow mooo-ved so she could see better. Everyone got presents, but Jesus got all the good stuff because He was the kid of the family!" Timmy stood with a big grin on his face waiting for the applause. The room broke out in chaos. Twenty-two children were all shouting different Christmas stories all at once trying to straighten Timmy out.

"Class, Class!" I had to shout over them to get their attention. "Wait, wait!" I said. Timmy looked crushed as he held his picture by one corner and let it fall to the floor. "Remember when we did the collages? When we took little parts of different pictures and glued them all together on one page to make a big picture?" They nodded remembering the fun we had. "Well, Timmy is so clever; he did the same thing with his painting of Christmas! He took parts of all the stories and put them together on one page!" I said smiling at Timmy.

"Oh!" the class exclaimed. "Let us see it again! Come on Timmy, hold it up higher!" they begged. Timmy happily complied and smiled over his shoulder at me as the other children pointed, and discussed his work.

"What is the TITLE?" asked one of the "accelerated students" who remembered we always try to name our special works. Without missing a beat, Timmy said proudly, "Scrambled Christmas!"

Perhaps there is a message here to consider in the presentation of a collage so carefully gathered. Life carries so much more meaning when we piece our journey together with thought and prayer.

CLASSROOM WITH HEART

JAY COOKINGHAM

For we are His workmanship, created in Christ Jesus for good works,
which God prepared beforehand that we should walk in them.

EPHESIANS 2:10 NKJV

He was a fifth grade teacher with a most unusual last name. He taught in a small middle school in upstate New York. I was a fifth grade student also with an unusual last name, who somehow landed in his class. I'm not sure if it was our "special names" that drew us together, but we hit it off from the very first day of school.

Mr. Coffee was one of those teachers whose charm was in the way he picked on you, never with malice but in a way that made you feel unique. Growing up my last name—Cookingham—was the source of many culinary comments (it still is to this day). When he found out my name he decided to give me an entire new nom de plume. I became the Baron Von Burnt Bacon, and I wore that title with a grin and pride.

Mr. Coffee learned of my family background, the situation of poverty I was living in, and for reasons unknown to me, he became my quiet benefactor.

Before I knew it I found myself being invited into his home, sharing meals and playtimes with his children. On certain weekends I slept over and often returned home with more clothes packed in my suitcase than what I had left with.

While being cheered on by his family I learned to ride a bike at his house, on his son's bike! My first favorite football team was the Dallas Cowboys, just because I watched the games on TV with him.

That summer he convinced me to let him sign me up for summer school just so I could go on all the special field trips he had planned, knowing full well it might be my only opportunity to see some incredible places like the Metropolitan Museum of Art. He knew I loved art and wanted me to see the Masters firsthand and possibly catch a vision for something greater for myself.

This kind man brought to our classroom an energy his name would suggest. I remember wanting to push myself to please him, to conquer each subject to try to measure up to the title of

Baron in his eyes. What I didn't realize was that I already had his approval; the real education was to prove to myself the potential I already held inside.

In that way he was a releaser of dreams, an advocate of pursuing those dreams, and I began to believe he was right.

I was too young to fully understand just exactly what was happening, but God was using a certain fifth-grade teacher to change my life. God used a secular environment to teach me more about His kingdom and my place in it. Although Mr. Coffee never mentioned the name of God, he showed the Father's love just the same. The manner in which he communicated values flowed through his gift as a teacher, and his life as a man.

God used that "classroom" to set a few points on my moral compass. This man's example helped establish my bearings on those points in life that God deems important: hard work, honesty, and caring for those around you.

Mr. Coffee seemed to realize the greater lessons in life are taught from the heart, not from books. His whole life was his classroom, not four walls inside a building. His example was not so much being a great teacher (he was) but being a great person when he taught. God was teaching and reaching through this humble spirit, and that made a huge difference in the life of a boy he nicknamed "the Baron."

GOOD MEDICINE: H₂O

GARNET HUNT WHITE

He healeth the broken in heart, and bindeth up their wounds.

PSALM 147:3

"W-H-A-A-A-H" pierced through the air. It was the second week of school. My insides shuddered. That howl set the pace for the kind of school day I could expect, as I knew the owner of that shriek; I had heard it every day the week before.

I closed my eyes and asked God to give me strength in coping with Debbie. *Dear God, I need Your help.*

A dull ache began at the base of my neck and upward through my head. *Why? Why did I follow in Mother's path and become a teacher?*

The bus driver carried a crying girl into my first grade classroom and said, "She says she hurt her finger."

"Hello, Debbie." I said.

We teachers did our own "doctoring." The school had no nurse and little money to buy first-aid supplies.

Debbie showed me her fingers.

"Let's wash your hand. Then we'll go to the yard and look at the trees in September."

Outside, Debbie stumbled over a rock, but didn't fall. She screamed, "My toe!"

"Let's go inside," I told the children; I led Debbie.

In the bathroom, Debbie pulled off her shoe and sock from the opposite foot that she stubbed; I washed it.

That afternoon, Debbie missed the handrail on the school bus. She shrieked. The bus driver hurriedly fastened my first graders' seat belts and headed the bus homeward.

The next two weeks, Debbie bawled about three times a day. When she cried, my headaches began. I decided to visit her parents; perhaps they could explain why Debbie cried so much.

I called Debbie's mother, Mrs. Deaton, and asked if I could come to visit after school. She agreed.

I arrived at Mrs. Deaton's house just as the school bus let Debbie off. She laughed, ran, and grabbed my hand. We held hands until we walked inside the house.

When Mrs. Deaton saw Debbie holding my hand, she threw a shoe at her daughter and said, "Get out of here! Get." Debbie ran from the room crying. "That's the meanest kid I ever saw. I wish I didn't have her."

I soon left Debbie's home, or was it a home? Debbie didn't have her mother's love, and she ejected her emotions by crying to gain attention.

That night, I discussed my troubling visit to the Deaton home with my husband, Glenn. I told him that I couldn't take the child's crying much longer and I felt like resigning from my teaching job.

"Go and resign; it isn't worth damaging your health. But remember, you've conquered situations worse than this before, and you always came out on top. You can overcome this chaos," Glenn said. "Debbie wants attention. Make her feel important."

"But how?" I asked.

"Oh, I don't know." Then he told me, "Use a fake medicine."

"Fake medicine?" I asked Glenn, "What?"

"Water. H_2O." And he went back to his reading.

The next morning, I filled an empty ketchup bottle with water, labeled it H_2O, and set it on my desk.

Debbie came into the room crying and holding her hand. I took her to my desk and bathed her hand in H_2O. "Does it feel better?"

She nodded and grinned, showing the absences of her front tooth; the tears magnified her large brown eyes, as they over-ran them and trickled down her cheeks to her mouth.

"This is your bottle of H_2O. When you get hurt, use it. If some of the children get hurt, would you rub your H_2O on them?"

Debbie turned to the other children, "Anyone hurt?"

Four raised their hands. Debbie ran to them and wiped their hands with H_2O.

The next recess Debbie came in bawling and holding her thumb.

"Put your H_2O on it." She ran to my desk and rubbed "her medicine" on the wrong thumb.

However, that day, Debbie's crying began to diminish.

When I saw Glenn that night, I thanked him for telling me about the "fake medicine." "God answered my prayers through you."

However, the glory of this cure nearly blew up the next morning after my class recited the Pledge of Allegiance to the flag.

Bart said, "Mommy said that H_2O was just water. She said you had Debbie doctoring with water. She said you're fooling us."

His cool, superior manner irked me. I looked at Debbie who seemed lost in her dreams. The other children turned their heads, stretched their necks, and looked at me.

That aggravation annoyed me as I stuttered for words to clear myself with my pupils. "Yes, Bart, your mother is right. That bottle has water in it. Doesn't about everything have water in it? Plants have to have water to grow."

My mind struggled to explain. "How many of you ate oats for breakfast?" Some hands rose. "Your mother put water in the oats before she cooked them, didn't she?"

"Yes," echoed from a few of the first graders.

"When your mother bakes bread or a cake, she puts water in the mix."

Eddie interrupted with: "Daddy buys our cakes and bread. He said they taste better than what Mommy cooks."

I then took my tray of apple slices and, as I passed them out to the pupils, said, "See how juicy this apple is as you eat it. That's water in the apple. Water makes the juice. What we eat has water in it; water's important."

I hadn't intended to give a home economics lesson that morning, but Bart spoke up and said, "My orange juice that I drink every morning has water in it."

"Bart, I'm glad you told the class about the orange juice, and you thank your mother for telling you about H_2O."

From that point on I had no more meddling about the medicine that Debbie used on herself and on her classmates. She continued to doctor herself and the other children with the H_2O, and her crying diminished.

Some of the children even began calling her Doctor Debbie, which pleased her immensely. She began to work harder on her lessons, took pride in class participation, and even helped the other students with their work.

As school closed the following May, Debbie ranked among my top ten pupils. Truly God had shown me the way to get through to this little girl and how to reach out to a young, troubled heart. And wherever Debbie may be today, I know His hand is upon her still.

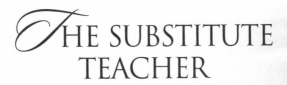

THE SUBSTITUTE TEACHER

MARGOLYN WOODS

For God is not unrighteous to forget your work and labour of love.

HEBREWS 6:10

The phone startled me.

"Could you possibly substitute for my class today?" asked my son's kindergarten teacher. "I have a family emergency, and I can't locate any of our regular subs."

As a stay-at-home mom, I was flattered. *How hard can this be?* I thought. *After all, it is only for one day.*

"Sure," I responded. After all, I had been in the workforce before I chose to be a stay-at-home mom. I hadn't been a teacher, but I had worked for fifteen years before having children. And, I did have three children of my own.

As I walked into the classroom, the bell rang. Before I could sit down, two sweet-looking little girls approached, "Can we go to the bathroom?" they asked.

"Sure," I said, not realizing the "one at a time" rule.

The morning started off relatively smooth. Then the teacher next door popped her head in the door and announced that the toilets were all stopped up. I now understood the "one at a time" rule and was off to find maintenance as she watched over both of our classrooms.

Lunch was an all time new experience. It was pizza day, and most of the kids at my table simply ate around the edges of the pizza, laughing at their milk mustaches from the chocolate milk. However, several opted to finger paint with the pudding, and they all wore some of their lunch back to the classroom.

The afternoon seemed to drag on as one child insisted it was her turn to be door monitor and another swore that it was his. I was beginning to realize the incredible talent it took to keep a classroom of children interested and excited about learning.

My son loved this class, and he loved Mrs. Winnie. Not only had she gained the respect of seventeen five-year-olds, but she had challenged them to follow inquisitive thoughts and sparked new interests.

I have to admit that I began watching the clock as it got closer to the end of the day. Not just to go home, but to sit down. I was exhausted! As the last child went out the door, I grabbed my coat and purse. Just then one small girl ran back inside. She threw her arms around me and gave me a big hug. "I love you," she said as she let go and once again headed for the door. My heart soared. I wouldn't have missed it for the world, but I was sure looking forward to going home.

And, as soon as I opened that door, I was going to put my feet up and write notes of appreciation to each of my children's teachers!

GOD LOVES US ALL

LINDA GILDEN

Not even a sparrow, worth only half a penny,

can fall to the ground without your Father knowing it.

And the very hairs on your head are all numbered. So don't be afraid;

you are more valuable to him than a whole flock of sparrows.

MATTHEW 10:29-31 NLT

"NO MAN HATES GOD WITHOUT FIRST HATING HIMSELF."
—Fulton J. Sheen

"Quick, come over here, hurry," Sarah Jane tugged at my hand. "Jimbo is about to break all the bird's eggs."

Bird's eggs? I wasn't aware that the children had found a bird's nest. They were usually so preoccupied with games of Dodge Ball and Chase that they never thought to even look for bird nests.

Walking toward the back of the playground, I heard a group of children yelling excitedly. I made my way over to the tree that nine-year-old Jimbo had shimmied up attempting to reach the robin's nest. He was doing his best to dislodge it from the branches.

"Jimbo," I said firmly, "leave the bird nest alone. Give the mama bird time to hatch her eggs." Inside the carefully built stick haven were three baby blue eggs.

Obviously, the mother bird had done an excellent job of positioning her home protectively. She just had not thought Jimbo would come along!

"Leave me alone," he shouted.

"Jimbo, do not break those bird eggs."

By this time recess had become focused on one thing: Jimbo and the bird's nest in the big tree in the corner of the playground. Several other children were trying to distract Jimbo from the nest. And before I knew it one of them pulled on his other leg; his grip loosened, and he fell to the ground with a thud. He got up swinging, determined to assert authority over the other children, as well as the bird's nest.

He flailed wildly, with no obvious target. He continued swinging as the children ran in all directions. Several, however, remained, and the brouhaha continued. Until he spun around and punched me in the stomach, that is.

Suddenly, movement was frozen, and there was dead silence. Hitting the teacher was definitely a no-no.

The rest of the group scattered, and Jimbo turned and sauntered off toward the classroom. His drooping shoulders, hands in his pockets, and low-hanging head acknowledged his mistake. Recovering from the shock of his behavior, I slowly walked toward the school. I had never had a student turn his or her anger my way. *How should I react?*

Mr. Brown, my assistant teacher, and I walked back together. "Would you take charge of the class for a few minutes?" I said.

"Sure," he replied, always glad to be in charge.

I walked back outside and around the corner. There was Jimbo sitting on the step with his chin resting on his hands. His body language did not welcome me. Without a word, I sat beside him.

The playground that had moments before been noisy and alive with children was strangely silent. I waited for the silence to become more comfortable.

After a moment I asked, "What made you want to do that?"

"Nobody cares about them little ol' bird eggs," he replied.

"God does."

"Nuh-uh, they're just lil' eggs. Nobody would miss 'em."

"You know God has a purpose for everything, even little bird eggs. He made the animals for a reason. And He really cares about them, just like He cares for you and me."

"Nobody cares 'bout me."

I looked over and saw Jimbo fighting tears.

"Jimbo, I do. And God does."

A tear escaped and made a dirt trail down his cheek.

He sniffed. "Ain't nobody ever told me that before."

"Jimbo, I love you, and I want to be your friend."

He turned his back to me so I wouldn't see the now steady flow of tears. I scooted closer to Jimbo and put my hand on his pulsing shoulder. He stiffened but didn't move away.

Lord, I have not been a teacher very long. I guess I didn't realize that some children don't even know You love them. Help me to love them all enough so they will realize how much You love them. Show me others in my class who need to know about Your love. And don't let me ever forget Jimbo.

I squeezed Jimbo's shoulders with both hands, and he leaned back against me.

We watched the mother bird fly back to the nest, obviously glad to get back to her soon-to-be brood. She fluttered and chirped and finally settled down.

I said, "Jimbo, you really are special to me."

A hint of a smile pulled at the corner of his mouth as we stood to go back inside. When I think about that day, I believe it to be a turning point in the life of a young boy, who just needed someone to care.

SO MUCH MORE

STEPHANIE CARLILE

In all thy ways acknowledge him, and he shall direct thy paths.

PROVERBS 3:6

As she walked up to my desk that morning I saw the usual piece of paper in her hand. *What now?* I thought, almost laughing to myself as she handed me the note. "It's from my mom," she said and went to her desk. I already knew that. The little girl's mother was well renowned throughout the school for sending daily notes and updates to her children's teachers. It was almost a joke now among the staff. She was like the postal system. Be it rain, snow, sleet, or hail—she was sending a note. This day was no exception.

I opened up the piece of paper and started to read.

Dear Miss Carlile,

You are so much more than a teacher.

You are an actress, a director, a decorator, a chef, a writer, an editor, a comedian, a referee, an athlete, a housekeeper, a doctor, a nurse, an artist, a storyteller, an electrician, a plumber, a parent, a saleswoman, a computer nerd, a motivational speaker, a cop, a singer, a carpenter, a manager, a planner, a scientist, a therapist, a coach, and most of all, a friend. You name it, and you do it. I just wanted to say thanks.

As a teacher, you more than likely will have a day when you wonder if you were cut out for this job. You will probably even have a day when you are on the verge of quitting. But remember how much you do for your students and how much you mean to them, and it all seems worth it! God has called you to be a teacher—be all that you can be. Let Him use you.

$\mathscr{A}$CUP OF COLD WATER

ELAINE YOUNG MCGUIRE

If anyone gives you even a cup of water because you belong

to the Messiah, I assure you, that person will be rewarded.

MARK 9:41 NLT

"NO ACT OF
KINDNESS,
HOWEVER
SMALL,
IS EVER
WASTED."

—*Aesop*

"Hic, Hic," reverberated off the yellow concrete block walls, and the noise seemed to bounce from one mobile to another that hung overhead. The sound was more annoying than a dripping water faucet at night.

Just as the room quieted and the students resumed answering test questions, there it would go again, "Hic. Hic." And I knew their concentration was flying away, right out the window.

It happened in my fifth period Bible class the year before I retired.

In my Christian school each student was required to take Bible classes and attend chapel every day.

Sometimes I worried that much of what I taught just didn't seem relevant to thirteen-year-olds, and, of course, their natural instincts seemed to rebel at anything they felt they were being made to do.

It was often difficult for them to identify with the lives of all the characters we studied—who had lived so long ago. Parts of the Bible seemed downright unbelievable to some of them. We learned about Sarah giving birth at ninety, of many people living hundreds of years, of old men courageously leading battles, and about thousands crossing the Red Sea on dry ground.

I was as old as their grandparents were. I posted rules and consequences, and most students behaved in my classes. We played games and did skits and activities to learn facts about the Bible and to remember the stories we read about. Sometimes I would tell them about my life and how God had helped me through hard times. They liked those days best, and, truthfully, so did I.

The school vision was to reach the hearts, as well as the minds, and I was required to teach the course from an academic perspective. I gave a lot of homework and expected it to be done on time and correctly. My students even had to do research projects.

Most students really wanted to do things right, but I know it was hard for them to keep up with my class, plus six others. I cared for them all and tried my best to treat them as individuals and to reach out to them, meeting their needs. But it was hard. After all, I had more than a hundred students and lots and lots of papers to grade.

I often played Christian CDs to start class but not typically the ones they preferred. I also kept a container of filtered water on my shelf to sip, from small cups, during a day of lectures. Most of my students weren't all that crazy about drinking water, but sometimes, on a hot day, especially after Physical Education class, my water could look mighty good to them.

Reflecting on that last year, I think the students liked the Bible class better when we studied the New Testament. I taught about grace and forgiveness, and we discussed the Good Shepherd. Often it was hard for them to see how it all fit together and even harder to see how any of it had anything to do with them. Living in a metropolitan area, they didn't know a lot about lambs or shepherds. When asked, they wished we could study more about how to help people or, perhaps study about how to make and keep friends.

My tests...well, they were long and very tedious. My students really had to concentrate to remember what they had studied. It was always hard to do, but especially the afternoon Kaitlyn got hiccups in class.

The school was strict, and Administration frowned on allowing the students to leave the room during test situations; so I couldn't just send her to the water fountain. Kaitlyn looked very embarrassed, and I could tell she thought I might be aggravated with her for interferring with the quietness and order of the classroom. The other kids were laughing every time she "hic-hicced."

I had always told the students about how the Bible had the answers to everything. And that day I prayed to know how to deal with the sound of hiccups filling the room.

Suddenly God gave me the answer. I walked to her desk, patted her shoulder, and put a little cup of water on her desk. She drank it, and the hiccups miraculously vanished as her body relaxed. It was the most marvelous thing. Not a word was said, but the entire class was quietly smiling. I was, too, and, even though Kaitlyn was extremely shy, she didn't seem mortified at all by the extra attention.

I think my students learned a lot that day. They will probably forget their grades or that they learned to name, in order, all the books of the Bible in seventh grade. I'm sure they won't remember all the stories or characters we discussed.

My students had wanted to know how to make friends and how to get along with others. This unplanned lesson taught them how to do that; smile, do good deeds quietly and when they aren't expected, and try hard not to embarrass another person. I learned far more than I taught that group of junior high students. I didn't have to do great things to make a difference in another's day. I could teach the Bible as an academic subject, give tests, and still touch tender hearts.

As always, I made mistakes here and there, but, in my heart, I know I taught Scripture by living it that one day. My immediate reward was in knowing the class learned I truly did care about each one of them, even though I had been a tough teacher. They could better comprehend stories about the worth of an individual to God. I think He became more real and approachable to us all.

The story of the Good Shepherd, who left the ninety-nine to go after one lost sheep, took on new meaning for all of us. And we easily recalled Mark 9:41. Even if we just give a cup of water to another, in His name, it is as if we are doing it for our Lord Himself. At that thought, I smiled at the memory of Kaitlyn's vanishing hiccups.

MADE PERFECT IN WEAKNESS

THERESE MARSZALEK

And He said to me, "My grace is sufficient for you,

for My strength is made perfect in weakness."

2 CORINTHIANS 12:9 NKJV

I don't want to go, I grumbled to myself as I prepared to whisk my kids off to school. It was the first Wednesday of the month, my day to volunteer in my daughter Emily's fourth-grade classroom. The temptation was great to reschedule or cancel my commitment altogether as numerous projects and looming deadlines cried for my attention.

While I silently searched for an excuse, my own words of wisdom quickly came to my remembrance. "You must always fulfill your commitments," I had preached to my children regularly. Being quick to repent, I refocused my direction for

"HOW COMPLETELY SATISFYING TO TURN FROM OUR LIMITATIONS TO A GOD WHO HAS NONE....FOR HIM TIME DOES NOT PASS, IT REMAINS.... GOD NEVER HURRIES. THERE ARE NO DEADLINES AGAINST WHICH HE MUST WORK. TO KNOW THIS IS TO QUIET OUR SPIRITS AND RELAX OUR NERVES."

—A.W. Tozer

225

the day, dressed myself with a new attitude, and planted a smile on my face.

On the short drive to school, I sought to surrender my will to God. *Have Your way today, Lord. I want to spend the day with You.* Little did I know that God was already waiting for me at school.

After receiving a warm welcome from Emily's busy teacher, I waited patiently for my assignment. "I'm really sorry," Mrs. Nagashima whispered, "I've got a really boring job for you today."

"Oh, I'd welcome a boring job!" I laughed. "I've been running so fast for the past several weeks that I'm worn out. I'd love a job that doesn't require me to think." Feeling the pressure of an increasing pace in both my professional and personal life, the thought of a mundane activity sounded pleasantly attractive to me.

Leading me to an empty classroom, Mrs. Nagashima instructed me to cover a stack of tattered reading books with construction paper. "You can work in here," she offered. "Or you can work in the volunteer workroom with the other ladies."

Seizing the opportunity to embrace some coveted time to myself, I assured her, "Oh, this will be just perfect right here."

"Ah," I sighed as I settled into the wooden school chair. "Peace and quiet." Suddenly aware of God's presence, I grasped the opportunity to talk openly to God.

Lord, I said, as I carefully cut and taped my first book cover. *I'm too busy. I've just got too much to do.*

Pondering the recent writing projects the Lord had given me, I began to express heartfelt gratitude—but my anxious thoughts quickly turned back to numerous projects waiting impatiently on my growing to-do list. Feeling my mounting stress return, I complained, *I'm grateful for doors You've opened for me, God, but there aren't enough hours in the day to get it all done.*

Thinking of my faithful husband and active family, I continued to pour out my unsettled heart. *The projects at church are such a privilege but so time-consuming...and on top of that there's the kids' sports, homework, cooking, cleaning, dinner guests, and out-of-town guests too. It's all important, and they're all good things but...I just don't know how I can do it all.*

God graciously allowed me to continue whining. Thinking about Bible college only two weeks away I continued, *And on top of that, Lord, You made a way for me to finish my degree...*

the classes, loads of homework, hours of study, and endless reading. How can I do it?

I sighed, worn out with anxiety. *Lord* I cried, dabbing the tears welling up in my eyes. *Maybe I've taken on too much… maybe I've missed Your direction. You know I've been notorious for getting overcommitted and burnt out.*

Completing my first stack of books, I looked up to Heaven. *Maybe I should put some projects off for a bit so I can catch my breath.*

Quietly setting my books down, I closed my eyes and waited in silence. Fully confident God understood my dilemma, I expected a comforting response from above.

As the growing silence became uncomfortable, I anticipated what God's response might be. *Oh, My daughter, you're right. What was I thinking? When you submitted yourself to Me, I guess I expected too much of you…I must have miscalculated how much you could handle.*

The long silence broke when God's loving words spoke to my heart. Quoting 2 Corinthians 12:9, He said, *My grace is sufficient for you, for my power is made perfect in weakness.* (NIV)

So much for sympathy.

God was right. Although I faced a demanding and pressing season of life, His grace and His strength would enable me to accomplish every task He had set before me.

Through my weakness, He is strong, I thought to myself as revelation settled in my heart. *I understand it now, Lord,* I said, feeling corrected, yet refreshed.

Yes, it would be humanly impossible to successfully complete God's work while maintaining a prosperous marriage, abundant health, and happy children; it would be impossible without God's help. I needed to receive His strength and His power.

God pulled me out of my fast-paced world and placed me in an empty classroom where I could slow down enough to hear His voice. I returned home from school carrying a fresh Heavenly revelation that changed the course of my life.

Approaching His throne as an empty vessel, I acknowledged my weakness and complete dependence on Him. God faithfully filled me with His ability to accomplish His ordained plan and enabled me to maintain a spirit of joy in the process.

Emily's grateful teacher was delighted with her newly covered reading books and carefully arranged them on the bookshelves for future use. When I visit Emily's classroom, I often glance toward that familiar bookshelf with a grin. The now gently used books remind me of the morning I met with God and discovered the treasure of His power in my weakness.

$\mathcal{S}$HE'S EARNED IT

MICHAEL T. POWERS

But those who came before us will teach you.

They will teach you from the wisdom of former generations.

JOB 8:10 NLT

Teachers do a thankless job for an obscenely low pay-check, and many times there are no short-term "rewards" as they are often left wondering if they are getting through to their students.

I would encourage you to make an attempt to write to those men and women who have touched your life through their gift of teaching. The simple act of a card or letter, even if you haven't seen them in twenty years, will allow them to realize that they have made a difference in the lives of their students. And hey, if you are currently a student, I'm sure it would be good for your high school or college career to let your present teachers know they are doing a good job! (That and a nice, big, shiny, red apple!)

231

Dear Senator Kohl,

I have had the privilege of knowing Karen Mullen, first as a teacher, and now as someone I have chosen to edit my first book. There is no one who prepared me more for college than did Mrs. Mullen. She encouraged my love of reading and writing, helped develop a love for classic literature through her choice of authors to study, and gave me some life lessons that I will never forget.

We did not just read a textbook, do homework on it, and get tested on the material in her classes. We were allowed to have open discussion after each story, sometimes veering away from the subject matter at hand, but always pertaining to something that we as students were interested in. She was tough but fair and earned the respect if not the love of all her students.

Most classes in high school I breezed through with a minimal amount of work. I rarely had any schoolwork that I took home. Not that our teachers didn't push us, it was just that I was able to figure out most of what was going on and finish assignments while the teacher was still talking about them. That was until I had Mrs. Mullen. I was nudged, stretched, and sometimes jolted out of my academic cruise control by her. For the first time in my high school career, I was working on assignments at home and most of those dealt with writing papers. We wrote papers, and then we wrote some more papers. I didn't appreciate her style of education until I got to college. After my first few weeks of university life, I was grateful for Mrs. Mullen. If it weren't for her classes in high school, college would have been a total shock for me.

Not only did she prepare me for college, she also changed my reading habits. Growing up, I had two genres that I read, and two only—epic fantasy, like *The Lord of the Rings,* and wildlife and outdoor fiction. When study hall came, I was usually caught up with my homework and would read for the entire period. During the first year I had her as a teacher in American Literature, I began to branch out and read the classics, but not just when we had an assignment. No, for the first time in my life I began to read Thoreau, Melville, and Poe for the pure pleasure of reading.

Toward the end of the first quarter of my senior year, my parents came to see Mrs. Mullen during one of the regularly scheduled parent/teacher conferences. I had straight A's that first quarter...or so I thought. There in front of Mrs. Mullen was a sheet of paper listing all the grades I was going to receive. Every teacher was giving me an A, except for Mrs. Mullen. She was giving me a B+ in her Psychological Literature class. Let me rephrase that. I was *earning* a B+ in her class. She told my folks that she felt bad that I wasn't going to get straight A's, but that I hadn't earned it. A B+, although close to an A, was still a B+.

My first thoughts were, *How much difference can there be between an A- and a B+? I was a good student, didn't get into trouble, and she couldn't give me an A, especially since straight A's would have been the result?* But the more I thought about it, the more I realized that I hadn't earned it, and that I would have to work harder the next quarter. That B+ stuck out like a sore thumb on my report card, but it was a motivating factor for me.

The following quarter, and the rest of my senior year, I earned straight A's. And the first one to come up and congratulate me was Mrs. Mullen after my second report card.

I leave you with a story I heard once that sums up my feelings toward my favorite high school teacher:

In ancient times a king decided to find and honor the greatest person among his subjects. A man of wealth and property was singled out. Another was praised for his healing powers; another for his wisdom and knowledge of the law. Still another was lauded for his business acumen. Many other successful people were brought back to the palace, and it became evident that the task of choosing the greatest would be difficult. Finally, the last candidate stood before the king. It was a woman. Her hair was white. Her eyes sparkled with the light of knowledge, understanding, and love.

"Who is this?" asked the king. "What has she done?"

"You have seen and heard all the others," said the king's aide. "This is their teacher."

The people applauded, and the king came down from his throne to honor her.

It is my hope that you also honor Karen Mullen. She's earned it.

Sincerely,
Michael T. Powers

Note from Michael: It is with great pleasure that I report that Mrs. Mullen did indeed win the coveted 2001 Kohl Foundation Teacher Award. Way to go, Mrs. Mullen!

MAESTRO

JAN WILSON

No discipline seems pleasant at the time, but painful.

Later on, however, it produces a harvest of righteousness

and peace for those who have been trained by it.

HEBREWS 12:11 NIV

"Play it again." His voice was soft and even. He cocked his head to the side, listening.

She played the piece again, smoothly in the beginning, stumbling over the middle portion and racing with relief through the last notes.

"You've made the same mistake each time. Can you find it and correct it?"

She sighed. This piece had plagued her all week. *Couldn't he just let it go?* She glanced at him seated next to her. The piano keys reflected off his thick glasses. *If I knew where the mistake was, I wouldn't have made it three times, now would I?*

When the correction was finally made, he moved on. Today it was scales. She sat playing a scale as he paced the perimeter of the room.

"Again."

She played again, more carefully this time.

"Once more."

What was the problem now? she wondered.

"I have an exercise I want you to do at home." Her fourth finger struck the notes with slightly less force than the other fingers. The exercise would strengthen the muscles to that finger and result in perfect scales.

"You're almost there, my dear," he said.

"Now pick out your favorite song for me," he said. He scraped the metal chair up to the piano again.

He huffed himself down onto the chair at her right elbow. His wool jacket brushed her forearm. The smell of mothballs filled her nostrils.

"Whenever you're ready, I'll follow you. Whatever you do," he instructed, "keep playing."

With a deep breath, she coaxed the music from the piano. He added higher notes to fill in.

"Keep going," he encouraged.

She repeated the melody with growing confidence. His harmony added depth to the piece. Midway, she slowed her fingers to keep pace with him.

"Once more!" The gray wisp of his hair bounced in time with the music.

The third time around, twangy notes distracted her. She would've stopped, but he shouted:

"Don't stop!"

Gloved in thin moisture, her hands skipped over the keys. He played like a sprinter crossing the finish line. She rushed to keep up with him. Thus ended her lesson on tempo.

There were some weeks that she barely practiced at all. Weeks when her Saturday lesson arrived and she hadn't prepared. She trudged into the room where he poured over the score of a Verdi opera like it was a juicy novel. Peering over the thick bifocals, he noticed that she hung her head, but he never questioned her. He cleared his throat and greeted her: "Well, there you are! Today we're going to do something a little different. Sit here," he waved toward a chair across the table. He walked to the piano and played a chord.

"Major or minor?" he asked. Several chords and correct responses later, her smile returned. He opened the book to the previous lesson, pressing the pages open with authority.

"Play this for me," he said.

She played with confidence. He closed the book.

"Play it again" he spoke slowly.

"I don't know it by heart. I need the music."

"Just try it."

She wrestled one phrase from her memory. Then another, and finally two more. Without any music, she played nearly half of the piece.

"You're almost there, my dear."

The next week, she bounced into the practice room. She plopped her book onto the music stand and pulled up the bench.

"What do you have for me?" he asked.

With a long breath, she forced her shoulders to relax. Then she slowly placed her trophy in front of him. The same piece, played perfectly, without seeing a note!

They examined the next lesson together. He shuffled through a cigar box on top of the piano. He retrieved the ancient pencil from the box and tapped the eraser on the page.

"What do you notice about this piece?" he asked.

"It looks hard," she said.

"Look again. See this chord? What is it?"

She picked out the notes in her head and pictured her fingers on the keys.

"It's a C."

"How many times does it appear in the piece?"

There were several. Then they searched for the F and G chords. The left hand seemed simpler now.

"You're almost there, my dear."

Years later, she lifted the rosewood cover of the piano, his piano. A loving torch passed on to illuminate the dark sorrow of his passing. The wrinkled page had defied her for three weeks. With a short pencil she grabbed from the music stand she circled the chords in the left hand. Just three of them.

You're almost there, my dear, she told herself, and smiled.

$\mathcal{C}$HILDREN TAUGHT ME TO FORGIVE

JOAN CLAYTON

As far as the east is from the west, so far has

he removed our transgressions from us.

PSALM 103:12 NIV

My students had been complaining all day, reporting instances of insults and mistreatment inflicted by one particular student.

Taking this one student aside, I tried to reason with her. To my surprise she vehemently denied any wrongdoing. When yet another student reported that she had pinched him, and the redness of his arm testified to the fact, I told her she would have to forfeit her recess until she could apologize.

She came in at the noon recess, sat down, and finished her math. The boy she had pinched had come in to finish his math also. They both brought their papers to me at about the same time. I checked them and said to her, "Do you have something to say?"

She quickly looked at the other student and sincerely replied: "I'm so sorry. I don't know why I did that. I wish…I really wish I wouldn't do things like that."

The boy patted her gently. "That's okay," he said with his chin quivering.

That ended it, with complete forgiveness, never to be remembered again.

The other children came in from the lunch recess, and we all settled down for story time on our reading rug. I noticed that my apologetic student hadn't joined us. She had offended so many other children, she was holding back, but deep down, I felt she longed to be included.

I pulled her close. "Do you have something you want to say to the other children?"

I breathed a sigh of relief as she came bounding forward. However, when she stood before the group, she remained silent with a hint of hostility. I asked her to please return to her seat and told her when she had something to say she could join us, praying all the while I had said the right thing.

I picked up my book and began to read to the children. As I read the last page, she came and whispered to the group: "I have something to say. I'm so sorry. I've been mean to you. I'm sorry I pulled your hair. I didn't mean to kick you. I'm sorry I spit on you. I really don't want to be that way!"

Spontaneously, the children cheered and clapped!

She smiled and nestled in among them. Even though the children had not mistreated her, they began to say, "We're sorry too. We didn't treat you as we should have."

Simple forgiveness had made things right. Other infractions of the rules would certainly occur, but that would be dealt with as they happened. This particular incident was closed forever.

What a lesson I learned that day. Instant replays of an incident that had happened months ago came to my mind. Every time I replayed it, I'd feel the unjust wounds, the same self-pity, and the same anger that festered in that unhealed place of my mind.

I was resolved that day and made a decision to forgive, to become childlike again in love and forgiveness. I also learned to look within myself. Like my students, I wanted to make things right, even if others might be at fault.

My students taught me the power of mercy. How thankful I am for a position that has allowed me to be with children.

"Of such is the kingdom of heaven!"

RIGHTS AND PERMISSIONS

MEET THE CONTRIBUTORS

Candy Arrington has numerous publishing credits; she also co-leads the "Writing 4 Him" critique and instruction group and serves as a judge for the 2004 *Writers' Digest* book contest. She teaches youth discipleship and is a choir member at her church in Spartanburg, South Carolina. She and her husband have two teenage children.

Esther M. Bailey is a freelance writer with more than 800 published credits. She is coauthor of two books: *Designed for Excellence* and *When Roosters Crow.* She resides in Phoenix, Arizona, with her husband, Ray. You can e-mail her at baileywick@juno.com.

Lanita Bradley Boyd taught school for thirty-four years. She enjoys reading, hiking, facilitating Bible studies, and traveling. She has been married for thirty-eight years, and has two children and one granddaughter. In her free time, she volunteers for Dress for Success, teaches ESL students, and directs women's classes and retreats for her church in Cincinnati, Ohio.

Annettee Budzban is an author, freelance writer, and religion columnist. She has been published worldwide on e-zines and in magazines such as *Guideposts, Angels on Earth,* and *Whispers from Heaven.* She can be contacted at ahrtwrites2u@aol.com

Renie Burghardt is a freelance writer with numerous credits in books, magazines, and online volumes. She loves nature, animals, reading, writing, and spending time with family and friends.

Stephanie Carlile graduated from Union College in Lincoln, Nebraska, and is the fourth- through sixth-grade teacher at Tulsa Adventist Academy in Tulsa, Oklahoma. She enjoys writing stories about her experiences in the classroom as a new teacher. Stephanie can be contacted at sjcarlile@yahoo.com.

Joan Clayton is the religion columnist for her local newspaper, and her newest release is a daily devotional. She has been included three times in *Who's Who Among America's Teachers.* She and her husband Emmitt reside in New Mexico.

Bradley S. Collins is a Substance Abuse Counselor who works primarily with at-risk men and women in Tulsa, Oklahoma. He also provides services and volunteers at treatment centers and other substance abuse recovery facilities, targeting persons affected by alcoholism and/or other drug addictions. Brad is happily married to his spirited wife, Debbie, and has a witty and fun-loving teenage daughter, Whitney. Brad can be contacted at Nolesdad@aol.com.

Lana Comstock has loved writing since childhood and picked up the hobby again just a few years ago. She has written for *Chicken Soup* and several other inspirational books. She really enjoys the written word.

Jay Cookingham is a freelance writer who has been featured on several websites, including www.fatherville.com, www.ibelieve.com, and www.christianwriters.com. His article "Seven Promises from Your Husband" was featured on two separate occasions on Ken Canfield's syndicated radio program, "Today's Father." He also writes a monthly e-mail newsletter geared towards men. His latest projects include a book on fathering and co-authoring a book on parenting with his wife, Christine. They have seven children blessing their home.

Ginger Cox worked over 25 years as a library-media specialist, receiving recognition as Teacher of the Year at her elementary school and as South Carolina's Media Person of the Year when she worked at a junior high school. Her photography and experiences in Israel, Europe, and South America add natural and cultural insights to Ginger's presentations and writing. She and her husband, Sam, delight in their two grown children's reunions at the family's 24-acre homestead (a house that Ginger designed and Sam built). Additional information is available at www.GingerCox.com.

Darla Satterfield Davis graduated from Southwestern Adventist University in north Texas, and has been teaching for fifteen years. She has been a contributor for *God's Way for Graduates* and *Make Your Day Count for Teachers,* as well as writing several articles for local newspapers. Ms. Davis is an artist, and the Owner/Steward of the Christian Fine Arts Center in Cleburne, Texas. She is available for speaking engagements throughout the summer months. You may contact Ms. Davis for more information at www.TheChristianFineArtsCenter.com.

Dr. C. Grant Endicott has been a freelance writer for the last twelve years, writing primarily for educational magazines and journals. He has traveled the United States as a conference speaker on subjects dealing with leadership and success as well as the development of organizational skills.

Nancy B. Gibbs, the author of four books, is a weekly religion columnist for two newspapers, a writer for *TWINS Magazine,* and a contributor to numerous books and magazines. Her stories and articles have appeared in seven *Chicken Soup for the Soul* books, *Guideposts* books, *Chocolate for Women, Women's World, Family Circle, Decision, Angels on Earth, On Mission Magazine, Happiness,* and many others. Nancy is a pastor's wife, a mother, and a grandmother. She may be reached at daiseydood@aol.com or by writing P.O. Box 53, Cordele, GA 31010.

Linda Gilden is the author of numerous articles, has contributed to thirteen books, and is the author of *Love Notes in Lunchboxes* (New Hope Publishers, 2004). A former kindergarten teacher, Linda and her husband enjoy spending time with their family where she finds lots of inspiration for her writing! Additional information is available at www.lindagilden.com.

Louise Tucker Jones is an award-winning author and inspirational speaker. Author of *Dance from the Heart* and co-author of *Extraordinary Kids,* her work is featured in magazines such as *Guideposts* and *Angels on Earth,* as well as a dozen compilation books. Louise resides in Edmond, OK. She may be contacted at: LouiseTJ@cox.net.

Eileen Key, freelance writer, resides in San Antonio, TX. She retired after teaching school for thirty years. Her publications are included in *Prayers and Promises for the Military, God Allows U-Turns, Looking Up* magazine, and various other places. She is an active member of Alamo City Christian Fellowship.

Melinda Lancaster is an author and minister who resides in Spring Hill, Tennessee, with her husband, Greg, and her son, Gregory. She enjoys reading, music, and writing poetry.

Muriel Larson has had seventeen Christian books and more than 7,500, first and reprint, writings and songs published. She has taught at various Christian conferences, writes a weekly column for the *Times-Examiner,* and, as "Dr. Muriel," counsels, via e-mail, thousands of worldwide readers of Campus Crusade's online magazines, *Christian Women Today* and *Women Today.*

Kathryn Lay is a freelance writer of more than 850 articles, essays, and short stories for children and adults in hundreds of magazines and anthologies. She is the author of three books for children and youth, and also serves as a writing instructor.

Patricia Lorenz is an internationally known inspirational, art-of-living writer and speaker. She's one of the top contributors to the *Chicken Soup for the Soul* books with twenty stories in fifteen of the titles. She's the author of four books, including her two newest published by Guideposts Books in March 2004: *Life's Too Short To Fold Your Underwear* and *Grab the Extinguisher, My Birthday Cake's on Fire.* Patricia raised two daughters and two sons and has had kids in college every year for the past sixteen years. She lives in Oak Creek, Wisconsin, and says she loves her empty nest and the freedom to follow her dreams while she's still awake!

Therese Marszalek is author of *Breaking Out* (Publish America) and co-author of *Miracles Still Happen* (Harrison House). Her writing has appeared in numerous publications across the country. She is a columnist, inspirational speaker, and instructor for Christian Writers seminars in the Inland

Northwest. She lives in Spokane, Washington, with her husband and their three children.

Janet Lynn Mitchell is a wife and mother of three. She is also an inspirational speaker and author of numerous articles and stories in several compilations. Janet can be reached at Janetlm@prodigy.net or faxed at (714) 633-6309.

Amanda Pilgrim works for White Stone Books and resides in Tulsa, Oklahoma, with her husband, Mike, and their many animals. She is a former educator and takes great pleasure in writing. She has been a contributor for both *Make Your Day Count for Teachers* and *God's Way for Graduates.* Amanda can be contacted at mayflowereditorial@cox.net.

Diane H. Pitts lives on the Gulf Coast with her husband and three rambunctious boys. She enjoys working as a physical therapist and writing for such projects as *The Heart of a Mother, God Allows U-Turns,* and *A Special Kind of Love.* Visit her at www.dianehpitts.com.

Michael T. Powers resides in Wisconsin with his wife, Kristi. His stories have appeared in eighteen inspirational books, and he is the author of the book, *Heart Touchers, "A Celebration of Life."* For a sneak peek or to join the thousands of readers on his inspirational e-mail list visit: http://www.HeartTouchers.com. You can email him at: HeartTouchers@aol.com.

Suzy Ryan teaches school and lives in Southern California with her husband and three kids. You can reach her at KenSuzyR@aol.com.

Gloria Cassity Stargel is an assignment writer for *Guideposts Magazine;* a freelance writer; and author of *The Healing, One Family's Victorious Struggle with Cancer,* published originally by Tyndale House Publishers. *The Healing* has been re-released in a special updated edition by Bright Morning Publications. Call 1-800-888-9529 or visit: www.brightmorning.com.

Lynda Blair Vernalia lives in Massachusetts with her husband, Drew. The holder of an EdM in Higher Education from Harvard University, Lynda has worked in retail, property management, and higher education and is now working to publish the thousands of poems and children's stories she has written since she was a teen. She can be found on occasion reading her poetry at Christian art festivals and local coffeehouses. Lynda can be reached at lbvern@attbi.com.

Garnet Hunt White is married to Glen E. White. A retired school teacher, she resides in the country on a beautiful, fifty-acre plot of land, where she takes care of orphaned animals dropped off at her home. She loves serving the Lord and attending church every Sunday.

Jan Wilson is the wife of one husband, mother to four children, grandma to one grandson—with another one on the way. She's been a RN for twenty-seven years and a Family Nurse Practitioner for nine years. Her writings have been published in the *Journal of Christian Nursing.* She facilitates monthly meetings of the Western Mass Christian Writers' Fellowship in Springfield, Massachusetts. You may contact her at www.scribesnscribblers.com.

Margolyn Woods lives in Oklahoma with her husband, Roy, and their three children. She is a popular speaker at women's retreats and conferences across the country, and the author of eight books. She can be reached at margolyn@cox.net.

Eileen Zygarlicke is an English teacher, freelance writer and youth coordinator for Hope Evangelical Covenant Church in Grand Forks, ND. Her passion is working with young adults and challenging them to make an impact for Christ in the lives of others.

ELL US YOUR STORY

*Can you recall a person's testimony or a time in your own
life when God touched your heart in a profound way?
Would your story encourage others to live God's Way?
Please share your story today, won't you?
God could use it to change a person's life forever.*

For Writer's Guidelines, future titles, and submission
procedures, visit:
www.godswaybooks.com

Or send a postage-paid, self-addressed envelope to:
God's Way Editorial
6528 E. 101st Street, Suite 416
Tulsa, Oklahoma 74133-6754

This and other titles in the God's Way Series
are available from your local bookstore.

Visit our website at:
www.whitestonebooks.com

*"...To him who overcomes I will give some of the hidden manna to
eat. And I will give him a white stone,
and on the stone a new name written which
no one knows except him who receives it."*

REVELATION 2:17 NKJV

WHITE STONE BOOKS
LAKELAND, FLORIDA